Unclutter Your Personal Life

Susan Wright

A Citadel Press Book

Published by Carol Publishing Group

A Citadel Press Book
Published by Carol Publishing Group
Citadel Press is a registered trademark of Carol Communications, Inc.

Editorial Offices: 600 Madison Avenue, New York, N.Y. 10022
Sales & Distribution Offices: 120 Enterprise Avenue, Secaucus, N.J. 07094
In Canada: Canadian Manda Group, P.O. Box 920, Station U, Toronto, Ontario M8Z 5P9

Queries regarding rights and permissions should be addressed to Carol Publishing Group, 600 Madison Avenue, New York, N.Y. 10022

Carol Publishing Group books are available at special discounts for bulk purchases, for sales promotions, fund raising, or educational purposes. Special editions can be created to specifications. For details contact: Special Sales Department, Carol Publishing Group, 120 Enterprise Avenue, Secaucus, N.J. 07094

Manufactured in the United States of America

10 9 8 7 6 5 4 3 2 1

Library of Congress Cataloging-in-Publication Data

Wright, Susan (Susan G.)
      Unclutter your personal life / by Susan Wright.
          p. cm.
      "A Learning Annex book."
      "A Citadel Press book."
      ISBN 0-8065-1466-3
      1. Home economics. 2. Time management. 3. Life skills.
I. Learning Annex (Firm) II. Title.
TX147.W96   1993   93-11591
640—dc20   CIP

Unclutter Your
Personal Life

Contents

CONTENTS

Introduction

Do you lack control over your life?

Do you spend most of your time thinking about your problems—health, money, chores, unfinished projects, relationships, boss—rather than pursuing your goals?

Do you have a lot of papers and possessions that you keep because you can't bear to part with them or because you think you might need them someday?

Do other people's needs and wants interfere with your life?

Do you want to do everything perfectly?

Then *Unclutter Your Personal Life* can help you. You'll get practical tips on becoming more productive by evaluating your goals and possessions. You'll also determine what your real needs and wants are, as opposed to what you think they are because of what others want.

There are two main areas of your personal life that you must learn to unclutter: your time and your space. This book is divided into two parts, one dealing with uncluttering your time, the other with uncluttering your space.

There are three steps to uncluttering each of these areas. First, you must define your overall goals and prioritize your projects. Next, you will eliminate the things you don't need, whether its objects, relationships, or obligations. Then you can create habits that will effectively help you reach your goals.

Cluttered Time

If your schedule is filled with tasks that aren't helping you reach your goals, then you have cluttered time. If you feel like you do nothing but work, but you still worry that you're not getting enough done, then you have cluttered time. If you find you're often late or miss deadlines, then you definitely have cluttered time.

You probably can't do everything you need to do and still have time for yourself. Time stress is created whenever you can't determine your priorities and negotiate the path between doing what you should do and what you want to do. Your time also becomes stressed by your desire to say yes to friends, family, and coworkers. Then there's the added stress of unexpected situations that inevitably come up in your life.

You're already making a conscious effort to manage your time—remember how hard it is to go back to work on Monday or after a vacation? That's because you have to summon the discipline to manage your time more strictly. You have habits in place to help you deal with your time—all you have to do is make sure your time management is the most efficient for you.

If you don't want life to be a never ending treadmill of work, projects, family, exercise, and household duties, then you must take control of your time. This book has practical tips that will help you determine your priorities and balance your life. You'll learn the difference between what you "should" do, what you want to do, and what you don't have to do.

Cluttered Space

No doubt about it—throwing away things you own involves a risk. Everyone thinks, "What if I need this later?" and "What about the feelings involved?"

It's difficult, but here's one promise: You won't ever get rid of something that's essential to your life. People who have problems with clutter are far too conservative as it is. Certainly by following some general rules to free your life of the confusion of clutter, you don't run the risk of going berserk and throwing out old family heirlooms.

The tips in this book are easy to remember, and since you aren't the organized type, you won't need to follow a schedule or tend to your clutter every day. Except for your desk and active work space, most of your clutter areas need to be examined only once or twice a year. Maintenance is easy when you learn how to stop clutter before it becomes a permanent part of your life.

You'll be surprised. You'll feel freer and more confident once you gain control of the things you own.

This book is for you if:
Your paperwork and files are a mess.
You are surrounded by clutter and don't know why.
You can never find a book in your library.
The contents of your closets are a mystery.
You are a confirmed collector.
Your house is disorganized.

Part One
Cluttered Time

1 | *Time Management*

Everyone wants to have control over his life. Instead, do you find you have too tight a hold on some things while you don't pay enough attention to others? Do worry and anxiety prod you along?

You may think it's impossible, but you can be focused enough to get everything done while being flexible and spontaneous enough to live.

Control over your life takes planning. Planning brings future goals into the present by enabling you to act now. When you are guided by overall goals, it's easy to determine what projects and activities to take on.

The key to time management is to do one thing at a time while keeping your overall goals in mind. That keeps you moving from one task or project to the next in a consistent direction.

First, you must determine your overall goals. What do you envision for your future? Be specific. Include lifestyle, career, relationships, environment, possessions, etc. These are your goals.

Each individual project in your life—whether it's redecorating your house, or completing a document for your job—should further you toward your overall goals. Don't waste time on projects that aren't helping you reach your goals. If you find you consistently take on certain activities or projects that have nothing to do with your overall goals,

3

then you either need to reexamine your goals or to be firm enough to say these things have no place in your life.

Once you decide to take on a project, then you must figure out the series of tasks that will best fulfill the specific goal of the project. Focus on each task and minimize interruptions. At the same time, always keep in mind the next task you intend to do. That will ensure a smooth transition from one task to the next, because the things you do tend to overlap naturally—you just need to be aware of it. Otherwise, you come to a complete halt when you finish a task and have to get yourself motivated to begin the next one.

The transition time from task to task and from project to project is important because it determines how well the entire process is flowing. As you work on a project, keep in mind:

- The goal of the project (what you want to accomplish) and why.
- The priority this project has in attaining your overall goals.
- The tasks needed to fulfill the goal of the project.
- The task you can do first, and a tentative sequence for the rest of the tasks.
- When you can realistically be finished.
- When you can start.
- Who can help you get this project (or specific task) done.

Time Is Precious

If you think it's not worth all the fuss to consider these things, then think again. You're cheating yourself of success when you mismanage your time.

Remember—time is more precious than anything else in your life, because unlike anything else, time is fixed. You can always get more money if you're broke, more friends if you have none, a new job....But we all race our lives against time.

So why do you allow others to waste your time? Why do you spend your time in ways you don't enjoy? Or ways that don't help you?

When you spend time doing something—anything—get something out of it, even if it's just learning to avoid such a situation in the future. If you're doing things that aren't pleasurable or worthwhile, then figure out why you didn't get what you wanted and how you could do it differently next time.

You may think that those few minutes here and there don't count for much. But look at it this way. Say you waste fifteen minutes a day. If you add up fifteen minutes a day for a year, that comes to ninety hours. That's ten nine-hour working days. Think of what you could accomplish in two weeks of work. That's what you waste when you waste those fifteen minutes every day.

2 | *Determining Your Goals*

The only way to make sure you are becoming the person you want to be is to envision your life in the future. Determine what you want from your life and work toward it. Be the type of person you want to be in the future. That's the way to accomplish anything, whether it's a successful career or a successful relationship.

This may involve a change in your life. Just remember that people don't really change—they transform.. You transform your life by taking a series of small steps, gradually shifting your attention and becoming more focused. You'll be fighting old habits, but most habits can be broken in just three weeks if you are committed and consistent. Three weeks isn't much when you're talking about a new start in life.

Determining your overall goals isn't something you do once and then you're through. Your future will in part be affected by things you can't predict right now. And through different stages of your life, you may develop different goals as your opinions, needs, and desires mature. Your effort isn't wasted when you find your overall goals have changed, because you always build on your past experience and successes. Keep evaluating your goals and your progress to make sure you're working toward the future you want right now.

In one way or another you've thought of your overall goals

your entire life. If you haven't articulated them to yourself and examined exactly what it is you want, chances are you won't fulfill them. It doesn't serve your best interests to allow you goals to be vague or to relegate them to daydreams. Tell a close friend or write down what you feel in a concrete and clear way.

What Do You Want?

You must know what you want in order to determine your overall goals. Your life goals, your goals for the next month, next year, or in five years will dictate the direction of your life. The goals you set must serve your own happiness; otherwise you won't be satisfied no matter how much you get done.

Write down what you would like to do or have. Be more specific than "success," "happiness," "love." Define exactly what those words mean to you. Include things you know it's not likely you'll ever do, like going white water rafting or traveling to India. Include things like a shopping spree at Bloomingdale's, a two-month vacation every year, eating an entire box of donuts while losing weight, or getting paid to do what you love. Write down everything you would like to do, or be, or have.

These things reveal a lot about you, and you may find you're not doing what you want with your life. Look for trends in your desires and ways that activities and projects dovetail. Is travel predominant? Do you want to control your own time or do something in particular? Do aspects of creating a home and having a family come up most often? Do you focus most often on your health?

Then ask yourself why you want these goals—whether it's objects you want to possess, or career success, or power, or money, or a certain type of relationship. Once you start to articulate your goals, you can analyze and refine them. This leads to understanding your own motivations, which can further clarify your desires. After all, if you're putting out all this effort, you might as well make sure you get exactly what you want.

Get Rid of "Should"

One thing to keep in mind when you're evaluating your goals is "should." When you say "should," you are glossing over the real reason you want to do or have something. Assumptions must be questioned in order to find the truth. For example, you tell yourself you should go to a meeting. Why? Because you've committed yourself? Because the people there expect it? Because that's what you've always done? "Shoulds" often indicate areas in which you aren't really thinking of what you're doing.

Whenever you hear yourself saying "I should" or "you should," stop yourself. Probe deeper and find out what you really feel about the situation. Also, when you hear someone else tell you that you should do something, ask the person why. You'll find out more about a person's beliefs by examining his/her "should's" than any other way.

3 | *Prioritize*

When you prioritize, you're deciding what is most important, what comes next, and what can wait.

Examine how you set your priorities—do they revolve around your own goals or others' goals? Only you can assess each activity's contribution to fulfilling your overall goals. If you don't structure your time needs to yourself, then you'll never be satisfied, even if everything eventually gets done.

A good way to determine which activities and projects have priority is to ask yourself, "What's the worst case scenario in my life if this doesn't get done?" The worst case scenario may not happen, but you want to make sure the things that have the potential to cause the greatest harm are given the top priority in your life.

Prioritize Individual Tasks

In any given project or activity, determine exactly what outcome is expected. If there is a set of specific goals you need to achieve, prioritize the goals as well.

Determine the tasks you need to complete in order to fulfill these goals. It helps if you envision the completed project. Then mentally work your way backward, noting down each step you would have to take to get the project done the way you see it. This will make it clear which tasks

9

you will have to build on the most. These tasks have greater importance than other tasks.

If there's an important task that you can do now, then do it. Most people tend to do the easier things first, as if building up to the most important task. But getting the big job done relieves the weight of its pressure that will otherwise hang over you as you do minor tasks. The object here is not only to get the job done, but to do it in a way that gives you peace of mind.

Set Priorities

You do have the time you need, you just need to make the right choices. When you set your priorities:

1. Do first what will benefit you the most. Why waste time with little return? Assess each situation and task according to its reward factor as well as to the damage it could do if left undone.

2. Once you make a decision to take action, don't allow yourself to be pushed into anything. If you have something more important to do, then do it without getting sidetracked.

3. Take care of the people who can help you or hurt you, whether it's your spouse or your boss, a customer or a coworker. The people who can most seriously affect your project should be dealt with first.

4. Take care of the things that have a time frame and won't last much longer. If you have a limited window of opportunity and it's something that you need, then it gets priority over the other, less immediate tasks.

5. Learn to tell the difference between what you

"should" do and what you want to do. Often what you "should" do is not what best serves you.

Act, Don't React

Many people prioritize by simply reacting to the situations that come up and adapting their schedules at the last minute. If you find yourself doing this, you're not managing your time, you're letting other people and other things manage it for you.

The easiest way to control your reactions is to focus on your own goals and the priorities you set. You need to rethink habits constantly and ask yourself why you feel the way you do. Don't let other people decide where you will go with your life.

If you find you aren't in control of something, then you have two choices: Get away from it or change your attitude about it.

You *are* capable of controlling the way you respond to things. Tell yourself you feel secure, confident, and positive, even if you have to fake it. Does that sound dishonest? It's simply an attitude adjustment. If you smile, it triggers an emotional reflex that makes you feel happier. If you believe you're confident, if you hold your shoulders straight and look people in the eye, then you will *be* more confident. Approach situations from a positive point of view and you'll be able to accomplish much greater things.

Also, confront your problems directly. Avoidance only prolongs the inevitable, but of course everyone instinctively avoids people and situations that make them uncomfortable. Next time you feel yourself drawing back or wanting to retreat, ask yourself what it is you're unwilling to face. Is it someone's approval you're seeking? Do you doubt your own ability? Does this reveal something you don't want to face in yourself?

If you have a problem, then admit it. Hiding your faults and the consequences of your actions, or pretending your problems don't exist, won't get you to your goals.

You are reacting to a situation instead of acting when you:

1. Solve each problem as it comes along, even if it interrupts a more important task or project;
2. Do the easy tasks first and build up to the harder tasks; or
3. Set the hard tasks to do first and let yourself get daunted by your work.

4 | *Other People's Expectations*

$\mathbf{W}$hen dealing with other people, you always need to remember that reality is not a fixed notion—it's each person's interpretation of what is going on, colored by that person's own unique wants and needs. Everyone has an idea of what will happen in any given situation. No matter how well or thoroughly you may believe you've done something, if it doesn't fulfill someone's expectations of what you should do, then it won't satisfy them.

You must learn to recognize other people's versions of reality and communicate clearly about both your expectations and theirs. While understanding others' expectations will help you determine if you are fulfilling their desires, don't allow their desires to pressure you into making someone else's reality your own.

Don't let anyone get away with making a vague or sweeping request. Make sure you understand what is wanted from you, so you won't be agreeing to more than you realize. If your boss gives you instructions for a project, clarify the goal as well as the deadlines. If your child asks for transportation to an event, clarify the time and number of passengers. With matters clear right from the start, there won't be a misunderstanding or disappointment.

Only after you understand what is wanted from you do you make a commitment. This is your time and effort you are agreeing to contribute, so don't feel pressured into doing it according to someone else's timetable. Be realistic about how long a project will take and always pad in extra time for the inevitable delays.

If you are running late, always let the person waiting for you or your finished project know before you are actually late. This notification will do more to alleviate anger from destroyed expectations on the other person's part than anything else. Your commitment has made the person happy, but it is the completion of your commitment that fulfills expectations. If you let the person know you will be late, he or she can then immediately form new expectations without having to dwell on the destruction of the previous one.

Whenever someone asks you to do something, ask yourself:

"How does this fulfill my overall goals?"

"What exactly do other people want or expect?"

"How can I meet the other person's expectations?"

"What can I realistically promise?"

Clarify

Make sure you listen to what other people say, so you don't hear what you *think* they're saying. If you don't understand them, you may end up doing something you thought they wanted or something that wasn't even needed.

You need to determine what exactly is being asked of you. Someone could be looking for your sympathy, your opinion, your support, your action, or just your company. If a person is looking for one thing and you give her another, no matter how well intentioned it may be, the person will be dissatisfied with you.

When someone asks you to do something, she may be more interested in speed than in the quality of your performance. Or it may be the other way around. You need to find out in order to satisfy the request without wasting your time.

One thing you can do is rephrase what you think the other person has said. Then listen to any modifications the other person makes to your words. This is the easiest way to clarify requests and suggestions.

You also need to be aware of body language. Many people don't know how to ask for what they really want. It is up to you to dive in and make sure it's clear to both of you. If someone looks pained or uncomfortable, she probably is. Find out why and how this affects the request.

Once you make a commitment, make sure the other person understands what you're prepared to give. Then keep your commitments. If you break a commitment, then make sure you tell the other person that you're aware of what you've done and will compensate.

Some things to remember when discussing projects or activities:

1. Don't assume anything
2. Ask questions
3. Be specific
4. Confirm the facts
5. Think before you speak

When someone is asking you to do a task or project, then make sure you clarify the following:

1. Your responsibilities
2. The limits on your authority
3. The results expected
4. When you are supposed to finish
5. The resources available to you (money, information, and materials)

5 | *Making Decisions*

When it comes to making decisions, it's sometimes hard to distinguish between what you want or need, and what others want or need. You also have to take both your long- and short-term goals into account.

Every time you make a choice, you are allocating your time. If every choice you make moves you closer to your goals, you'll get there a lot faster. But you may be making decisions based on some extraneous ground, such as:

1. **Habit.** When you do something over and over again without thinking, it's difficult to see that you are trapped in an unproductive behavior pattern. Often other people can point out habits we aren't even aware of. Listen to your friends and family, and determine if your habits help you advance toward your goals.

2. **The demands of others.** You may find it easier to give in to the requests of other people than to say no when you would like to, but ultimately you are not serving your best interests when you do. In the long run, it serves everyone for you to make your own decisions even if the people in your life don't like them.

3. **Fear.** When you consider doing something, and come up with all kinds of reasons why it's impossible, then you're letting your fear make

your decisions for you. You have to get past your
fears to achieve your goals.

4. **Impulse.** The desire to do something just for the
sake of doing it can prompt you into activities that
don't help you toward your goals.

5. **Inaction.** When you wait for others to come to
you with options, then you're putting your own
life on hold.

Learning to Say No

Most people want to make other people happy, but it's
better in the long run to say no than to settle for the
temporary relief of making a commitment that you won't be
able to keep. When you can't fulfill a commitment, you're
left with a disappointed boss or spouse and the accusation
that you are inconsiderate or uncaring.

Learn to break the habit of always thinking that others
need you or that "no" is rude or selfish. You and you alone
set the boundaries of your actions, and the sooner you take
responsibility for that, the sooner you'll stop letting others
tell you what to do.

By learning to say no without having to justify yourself or
feeling guilty, you reclaim your time for your own to do
with as you want. It's not justification to say that you have
time constraints or a prior commitment—if this is true,
then you're simply making your refusal more understand-
able to the person. But don't feel you need to create a reason
for you refusal, or offer a long explanation.

Ways to Say No

There are ways to say no that will keep you from feeling
selfish and will satisfy the other person at the same time.
For example:

1. Offer to do the project or join them for an activity

at another time. This way, you can say no without others feeling completely rejected. If your sister asks you to come shopping, simply tell her that you can't right now, but perhaps you could on Friday or next week.

2. Suggest someone else who may be able to help. If it's a business situation, you can offer to ask a coworker if he or she can do the job. If it's personal, you can suggest another friend who may not be busy.

3. Offer to get back to the person if you need time to think it over. You can always request time to consult your schedule when someone asks you for something. This will give you the chance to determine if you can realistically meet the request and what tack to take if you decide to refuse.

5. Offer to do some of it. Negotiation is always possible when someone requests something from you. It may be you don't understand part of the request, and by discussing the aspects you aren't willing to do, you may find the request isn't what you thought it was.

When someone asks you to do something, pause before answering. You never benefit yourself or others by rushing to comply. Give yourself time to think about the request and find out more if there is something you don't understand. If something is telling you to say no, then listen to yourself. Then say no effectively, by being clear about why you are saying no and considerate of the person requesting your time.

When to Say No

Here's a few handy hints about when to say no:

1. Don't give anyone what you wouldn't ask for.

2. Say no to everything that is against your principles, morals, or best interests.
3. Say no to anything that is inconsiderate of you.
4. Say no when someone asks you to do something that he can do for himself.
5. Say no when someone asks you for a favor and specifies conditions as to how you're to fulfill the request.
6. Say no when someone asks for more than you've offered to give.
7. Don't allow people to insist or argue with you after you have said no. Simply say, "I've already said no."

6 | *Time Wasters*

Do only one thing at a time. Do it as quickly as you can according to the standards necessary to fulfill the goals of the project or your overall goals. Then immediately move on to the next task.

When you start dividing your attention and try to deal with things as they occur, you lose your focus. The most efficient way to achieve your overall goals is by concentrating on each individual activity or project and carrying it through to completion.

Interruptions and How to Limit Them

One way to maintain your focus is by limiting interruptions. If you can acquire this skill, you'll get through all your projects quicker and more efficiently.

Unexpected things will always happen, but that doesn't mean you take care of them whenever they come up. You also don't owe it to anyone to give them your time when you're committed to something else. You can always let people know in an effective and polite way that they are interrupting you.

The telephone is a terrible interrupter. When you plan to work on a project, control your calls by letting an answering machine screen the messages. Don't return calls until you have completed the task you have set.

People also tend to interrupt by dropping in when you are at your desk or home. In your home, family members often believe they have the right to interrupt you just because you're there. Emergencies do happen, but more often than not, interruptions are simply situations that destroy your focus.

Ways to Limit Interruptions
Learn to limit interruptions by recognizing them for what they are. Handle interruptions in a way that will prevent them from occurring again. A few ways to do this are:

1. Set a time limit on the conversation. When someone interrupts you, tell her you'd love to help but that you only have a minute to spare. It's a polite way of not shutting the door in a person's face while letting her know you are busy.
2. Make an appointment to see the person later. In business, it's always best for you to control the time and setting of a meeting. In your personal life, both you and your family will benefit from knowing a time has been set aside for you to be together.
3. Request that distractions cease—whether it's actual interruptions or loud noises that rob you of your focus. Often, people don't know they're bothering you until you let them know in a considerate, polite way.

Telephones

It's always better to make a call then receive one, because the person making the call controls the start of the conversation and is better prepared to limit its content and length. Make sure you think about what you need to get done before placing the call.

If used correctly, your phone calls can save a lot of the time you would ordinarily spend in traveling to meet someone or to buy things. Whenever possible, make your arrangements and contacts over the phone. And use the phone and your credit card to buy tickets, order flowers, groceries, gifts, etc. Using the phone can also be useful because you can often do something else while you're talking, such as ironing, straightening a drawer, filing your nails, cleaning out your wallet, folding laundry, etc. A long telephone cord, a speaker, or a cordless phone will give you added freedom of movement.

Rather than being available at all times, you can give people a specific time-frame when you talk on the phone, whether it's early afternoon or after dinner. Determine when it's best for you to make the majority of your phone calls.

When you want your business calls to be quick, then it's good to call right before lunch or before the end of the business day. Most people will be anxious to get the important part of the conversation done so they can get out the door.

Taking Control of Your Phone Calls
Some ways to do this are:

1. Leave your answering machine on to screen calls.
2. Make your outgoing calls together in a block of time.
3. Return calls rather than answering when someone else calls.
4. Leave detailed messages so the other person is prepared to discuss your concerns.
5. Develop conversation enders, such as:
    What can I do for you?
    You must be busy, so I'll let you go.
    Is there anything else?

Before we hang up....

I've got someone here (or on the other line)...

6. Be aware of the time you spend on the phone. Consider prior to the call how long you want it to last.

Conversations

When you get drawn into a conversation, discuss the topics that are important to you. If things wander off aimlessly, be direct and ask for clarification of an earlier point in the conversation. From there, it should be easy to bring it back to the topic you want.

A good way to end a conversation is by using the "Yes, but..." technique. Affirm what the other person is talking about, then add the "but" to indicate your need to end the conversation. A few examples are:

1. That's interesting, but I won't be able to get to it until later.
2. I'm glad you told me about this, but right now I have to concentrate on something else.
3. That part I understand, but what I need is...
4. You've got a good point, but I can't talk about it right now.

An even better way of ending a conversation is to affirm the other person, while convincing him it's in his best interest to end the conversation. A few examples are:

1. I wish I could help, but then we'd have twice as much to do tomorrow.
2. That's interesting, but we're going to lose a customer if I don't go now.
3. I'd like to talk to you longer, but we'll miss our deadline.

Then make the first move. Don't wait for the other person to leave. Reach out and shake his hand if he's in your area. Start around your desk or walk toward the door to show him out. Walk briskly away if you have to.

Meetings

The next time you call a meeting, don't make the mistake of wasting valuable time.

1. Determine exactly what you want to accomplish in the meeting and set objectives. Write down the key points and keep track of your progress during the meeting.
2. Assign information-gathering to coworkers and be clear about what you need from their reports. Make sure these people are available for your meeting time.
3. Start on schedule and take notes on decisions, information, and solutions to possible problems.
4. Keep your reports on track. It's up to you to cut digressions before they get out of hand. If one person is having trouble with the discussion, tell her you will meet with her privately afterward and deal with the questions then.
5. Don't include people who aren't necessary. A summary can be distributed to interested coworkers who don't need to be involved in the decision-making process.

When you aren't the one who called the meeting, it can sometimes be difficult to implement these steps. But your suggestions to keep the meeting on track will be noticed and appreciated.

If you can't take control so easily, then make sure you have other work you can concentrate on when the meeting doesn't directly concern you. If your boss comments, point out how important your current task is, while the topic under discussion doesn't have any bearing on you.

Another tactic is to arrive on time but request to leave early. It's much better than arriving late.

Other Time Wasters

Here are some additional tips on how to avoid assorted time wasters.

1. Consolidate your errands and plot out your path to minimize travel time.
2. Don't stop to answer to "just a few questions." Unless you are applying for something you want, don't waste your time filling out applications and questionnaires that other people give you.
3. Throw away junk mail. Whatever you do, don't waste time reading it.
4. Worry is one of the biggest time wasters. If you think about a problem but are unable to solve it, stop thinking about it. The next time you think about it, you may have an answer for the very reason that you left it alone.
5. Know when to cut your losses. If something isn't working and hasn't been working, then the situation needs reworking. The rule of baseball is pretty good in most situations—"Three strikes and you're out."
6. Don't cry over spilt milk. Getting upset or depressed about a problem accomplishes nothing. When you tell yourself, "I told you so," you are undermining any action you could be taking right now to make things better.

7 | *Managing Your Time*

Did you know that when you work, one-fifth of your effort will produce 80 percent of the finished product?. The other four-fifths of your time are spent on things that take much more time with far less result. Obviously, choosing which tasks to do is very important.

Other real-live examples of the 80/20 ratio are:

80 percent of sick leave is taken by 20 percent of employees.

80 percent of production is in 20 percent of the product line.

80 of sales comes out of 20 percent of customers.

80 percent of TV time is spent on 20 percent of programs.

80 percent of dirt is on 20 percent of floor area—the part most frequently used.

Remember this 80/20 ratio when you get caught up in trying to get everything done. What's important is choosing the critical 20 percent of your activities that produce the biggest yield, then whatever else you get done on the remaining 80 percent is already building from a substantial base.

Write It Down

Don't rely on your memory to keep track of your goals and commitments. Write down your plans, goals, and priorities, as well as potential activities and deadlines. You already have too much information constantly coming into your life to keep everything in your head.

Since most people plan out their time in weekly increments, the best calendar to use is one that shows a week at a time. Daily calendars force you to flip back and forth between five or six pages as you try to plan your week. Details tend to disappear in all that page turning.

A monthly page is useful for plotting out the major details, but if you're a busy person, most monthly calendars don't include enough space to be practical for all planning needs.

The most important thing about your calendar is to get in the habit of referring to it constantly and keeping it updated.

Lists are a good supplement to your calendar for daily tasks as well as for plotting out your overall goals. As you complete tasks and activities, you can cross them off the list. It's an act of self-affirmation, confirming that you are coping with the tasks in your life. Instead of thinking of the things you haven't done yet, you can take pride in the ones you've completed.

Update your list as you go along. You may find that every few days the completed tasks outweigh the ones left. Then you can make a fresh list. Prioritize the list as much as possible. And for the sake of clarity, separate the "To Do" activities from the "To Buy" and "To Call" entries.

Delegate

If something can be delegated, then by all means delegate it. Don't hesitate because you don't like to ask for help, or because other people will think you can't do it on your own. If you do everything for yourself, then your production is limited to what one person can do. Whatever keeps you from delegating responsibility is keeping you from accomplishing greater things in your life.

You can organize, direct, motivate, and get the job done the way you want. This includes your personal life as well as business. Assign responsibilities, make sure you're kept posted if the task is of long duration, and then leave the other person to complete it. You don't need to be looking over her shoulder to make sure it gets done.

The best way to delegate is to ask, not force a person to help you. You want her to want to help you—that way she can give her talents fully to the task. You must motivate others to help you, and to do that you have to understand what the other person's priorities are. Security? Attention? Promotion? Money? Fun? Esteem? Success?

Most people aren't even fully aware of what motivates them. You can only watch habits and patterns and determine as best you can what outcome each individual is most satisfied with. Keep an open mind, because people are much more complicated than they appear to be. Assume that their intentions are good and don't judge someone else on the basis of your own goals. The trick is to give people what they want, while making sure you get what you want.

When you delegate tasks, make sure the other person understands:

1. Exactly what you want.
2. What she has to gain from doing it (addressing her priorities).
3. How much authority she has.
4. What resources she has access to.
5. When you want the job done.

These five points need to be discussed thoroughly. Listen to the other person's opinions and ideas about the task. If you think something can be done in two days and your coworker tells you it will take three, she may be aware of details that you aren't.

In accepting a commitment from someone, make it clear that:

1. The deadline you've agree upon is important.
2. You want to hear about any problems that may interfere with completion of the task on time, as well as possible solutions to the problem.
3. If you don't hear any reports, then you'll assume that the project or task is progressing well and will be done on time.

Padding Time

Always pad your time estimates. Few people will ever notice if you request an extra fifteen minutes to drive to an appointment, or an extra few days to complete a project. But people always notice if you're late, because you're keeping them waiting. In effect, you are wasting their precious time and causing more stress for them.

Besides, constant rush contributes more to your "time stress" than anything else. Why push yourself to make a deadline when you can relieve all pressure by making it a habit to pad your estimates? Again, this works whether you're trying to make it to the dry cleaner before it closes or get to work on time.

Building time in is even more important where others are involved. You must allow for the inevitable delays because you can't be sure that they will. When you give someone a deadline, make sure it's earlier than you really need it—but don't let the other person know that.

Contingency Plans

No matter how good you are at streamlining your life, scheduling your projects, or minimizing interruptions, things will always happen to complicate your life. When a problem comes up, you have to be flexible with your schedule. If you plan your time too tightly, you'll end up frustrating yourself and working far more hours on projects than you want to.

These are a few techniques for developing contingency plans:

1. When a problem develops, there are probably things on your schedule that don't have to be done right away. You can delegate these tasks or put them off for a while to deal with the high-priority tasks.
2. Don't schedule things for the last minute. If a project is to be done on Friday, then plan to get it done by Thursday. That gives you a whole day's grace period.
3. Do the most important task first. That way, if something does develop that interferes with your schedule, you've already covered a key area and your entire project won't suffer.
4. Renegotiate deadlines. Often, deadlines aren't hard and fast—they're simply expectations. If you discuss a change with the person expecting the project to be done, you may find you'll be able to extend your working time in order to get the job done well.

8 | *Procrastination*

People procrastinate for all sorts of reasons. Evaluate each situation to determine what is keeping you from getting started. Sometimes, all you need to do is recognize a certain pattern in order to form new habits. The following are some tips for when you find yourself faced with a project that you just can't seem to get started on. Try one.

Manipulate Time

One simple trick often works. Record the due dates of projects and appointments on your calendar a little earlier than they actually are. If you have a meeting at 1:00 P.M., record the time as 12:45. If a report is due Monday, note that it is due Thursday or Friday.

Even though you may remember that you have a few extra days or minutes, the psychological impact of seeing an earlier date will help speed you along. Also, try telling yourself that the early time is correct and forget you have extra time. This will keep you from delaying the start of your project until the weekend before it's due.

Another, similar method is to set arbitrary deadlines for yourself. Tell yourself that you must write that letter by Thursday, or by eight o'clock this evening.

Render the Task Into Smaller Pieces

Break down large tasks. It's easier to face a score of little tasks than one enormous one. It won't take less time, but if your problem is procrastination, you may be able to trick yourself into doing several of the small pieces of the task, and so have tackled it before you realize it.

Sometimes all it takes is one movement forward to break the barrier of procrastination. Find the easiest part of the task and begin with that. It doesn't matter if that particular part does not need to be completed until the end of the project; if it gets you going, that's all you need. Just as directors often shoot films with the scenes out of sequence, many unwieldy tasks can be handled in the random sequence.

Don't wait for a huge block of time to do the entire project. If you have to organize your library, do whatever can be done in little blocks of time. If the project will take weeks or months to complete, you may need to break it into sections before you start; thus, you allow yourself a series of small successes or completion of parts instead of waiting for overall success on completion of the project as a whole. These small successes also give you a second wind for the next stage of the project.

Stop Being a Perfectionist

Sometimes your standards are too high. If your standards make a task seem overpowering, you may never get around to doing it. Don't aim to be perfect; aim to get the job done. If you are a perfectionist, then figure your habits of polishing the work will kick in later. Don't think about it at the beginning or you'll worry yourself right out of the ballpark.

If you can't take a step for fear of going in the wrong

direction, take that step anyway. Just as most writers throw away their first page or first chapter, the preliminary steps are sometimes important simply because they help you realize what direction you need to go in.

Sometimes, too, the only thing you can do is give in to the inevitable. If you must procrastinate, don't do *anything* else for at least fifteen minutes. Don't read, don't talk to anyone, don't take phone calls. After a few minutes of doing nothing but thinking about that project waiting for you, you'll do anything to get it going.

Unpleasant Tasks

Sometimes people procrastinate because a particular task is unpleasant. From childhood you learn that if you ignore things you don't like to do, someone eventually comes along and does it. Or else you are forced to do it by an adult. This creates a harmful pattern of relying on something or someone else to get work done. Ask yourself if this is your problem, and if it is, become your own adult figure.

Whenever possible, delegate tasks you don't like to do. That will ensure that they get done while at the same time freeing you from having to do it.

If you must do an unpleasant task, reward yourself when you have finished. Rewards can be anything from a fifteen minute break, to buying a new book, taking a walk around the block, or treating yourself to a snack. The carrot almost always works better than the stick. Even if you've never thought of rewarding yourself with an hour off, try it when you're faced with a task you dread that you can't avoid.

Is there one type of task about which you procrastinate on a regular basis? It could be a work environment problem. When you have to write letters, your typing equipment may be hard to set up; when you have to pay bills, the phone may be constantly ringing. What you consider to be a difficult task could really be a bad environment for performing that task.

Look Beyond the Task

If nothing works to get you started, perhaps there are deeper reasons why you are procrastinating. Ask yourself why you haven't written to your mother-in-law or called the travel agent about vacation plans. The most simple tasks can sometimes be the ones fraught with the most emotional tension. Coming to terms with that tension may be more important than getting the task done—and it may be the only way the task gets done.

Part Two
Cluttered Space

9 | *Coming to Terms With Clutter in Your Life*

People save things because it gives them a sense of control over life. When you gather possessions, you are reassured of your power to acquire what you need every time you look around your house.

Saving and collecting objects is not bad in itself, but possessions can become a crutch, replacing inner confidence with an outer manifestation of security. That, in turn, makes you more vulnerable. Your possessions can be lost or stolen or burned in a fire. If this thought terrifies you, then maybe it's time to work on your attitude toward your things.

It's easy to attach sentiment to things simply because you own them. But you own a lot of things, and have in the past, and will own more in the future. Everyone's life is a huge cycle of owning and throwing away. Just because something belongs to you, doesn't mean you're supposed to keep it for the rest of your life.

Find something right now that you don't use. An old magazine, a clipping you were saving, a dust covered jar or knickknack. Now throw it away. If you have trouble, you're probably investing the object with false importance.

With some simple techniques, you'll be able to cull the dead wood from your life. Then, without needless clutter and with your possessions handily organized, you won't have to spend as much time thinking about the objects in your life. Your possessions will stop getting in your way. And you will no longer have to deal with thoughts of "I should clean that closet" or "I'm so embarrassed that people see my house like this."

Remember that clutter often consists of relics from your past that no longer reflect who you are today. Many people are reluctant to give up the symbols that used to define them. But in order to create the future you want, you must create an environment that reflects who you want to be—not who you were.

What Is Clutter?

Clutter is anything you don't really need in your life. Clutter takes up space and time and keeps you from having room for things you do want.

Here are a few examples:

1. Clutter is what you aren't using.
2. Clutter is useful objects that don't have a specific storage place.
3. Clutter is unrelated things mixed in with useful things.
4. Clutter is unfinished business.
5. Clutter is anything that gnaws at you.

Like cluttered time, cluttered space is *unspecific*. You must mange your space, assigning a use to each area of your home and to your work surfaces.

The Biggest Clutter Traps

"I might need this someday."

Beware of these thoughts: "I might need this some day," "This might come in handy." If you think this when you pick up an object, then immediately get rid of that object. It's clutter. In fact, most clutter in your house is masquerading as something that's potentially useful.

"I got it as a gift."

When it comes to gifts, remember the old adage, "It's the thought that counts." If you don't use it, and it won't be missed, give it away or throw it out. The caring and thought that went into the gift is enough in itself, no matter if the gift is perfect or if it doesn't suit you at all. Don't keep that enormous juicer if you're allergic to citrus or if you already have two others. Don't add to the clutter in your life out of a false sense of obligation to keep everyone's gifts to you.

"It's still perfectly good."

But do you use it? If the answer is no, then get rid of it even if you have to throw away a fully functioning lamp or recliner.

"It will be worth money someday."

How do you know? And will you still be around to collect? Do you want to bother holding boxes of baseball cards or comic books just to make a few hundred dollars at some undetermined later date?

"It's a souvenir from..."

Unless an object fits the environment that you decide best reflects *you*, don't save it. Don't give in for the sake of memories. An object can't replace your memory, even though people so often place the value of the experience in the object itself.

"I paid good money for this."

You've paid money for lots of things that still aren't in your life. Just because you own something doesn't give it inherent worth.

"It just needs a little fixing."

But if you don't get around to fixing it, then it's useless and should be thrown away. Don't make projects for yourself that aren't important.

I've had it a long time."

Usually when you say this, you don't even consider that the object could be clutter. After all, it's been around so long it must be necessary to your life...right? You may even think the object is interesting in and of itself. But even if it once was useful in your life, if it doesn't serve as a reflection of who you are today, it's time for it to go. Just remember that the object is keeping something else—something that reflects who you want to be—from taking its place. The more specific about who you are and what you want in your life, the easier it is to decide.

Mementos

Objects that retain some sort of sentimental value are the most difficult kind of clutter to eliminate. Does the object have value because you owned it during a certain period of your life? Does it remind you of a friend, a lover, a relative? Or do you value it because at one time you really wanted or liked the object and now having it has become a habit?

Many of the possessions you place sentimental value on can be eliminated without depriving you of your memories. After all, it is the memory that's important, not the objects.

First, consider how many other objects you have that remind you of that person or place or time in your life. If you have dozens of keepsakes from old friends or lovers you hardly ever think about, then get rid of them. These objects are reminders of your past when you need to be concentrating on your future.

Childhood relics are also hard to get rid of. Don't throw everything away, but consider the objects together. Which are more important and why? Do some of the objects represent important steps you took in your life? Are they early indications of what you wanted from life? Keep those and get rid of the ones that were simply possessions.

You don't have to throw away all of your memento clutter at once. If you go through your stored objects every couple of years, getting rid of a few items here and there that you've realized aren't as important as you thought, then you'll gradually whittle down your unused possessions.

10 | *The Process of Eliminating Clutter*

The hardest part of eliminating clutter is the decision you must make with every object. But how can you decide if something is clutter without spending a lot of time? Most people keep things simply because they fall into a nebulous "maybe" area, and it's easier to stick the object someplace than to deal with the issue of whether you really need it or not.

Consider Each Object

Since clutter is a mass of jumbled things, it's easy to become daunted by the task. But like any other project in your life, you get more done if you concentrate on one thing at a time.

1. Pick up each object and ask yourself if you use it. Do you use it frequently? Seldom? Never? Throw it out if you don't use it or use it very seldom. Only keep objects that you *use.*
2. If you do use the object, then designate a particular storage area, easily accessible or not, according to how often you need it.
3. Store objects with similar objects—office supplies together, mailing supplies in one drawer, sewing materials together, etc.
4. If the object is an unfinished project that you've

been saying you'll get back to—face your procrastination. Either throw it out or set a deadline of a week or a month, depending on the size of the project. If you don't finish it in that time, then get rid of the unfinished business.

5. Don't let objects cause you stress. If something is bothering you—a messy closet or drawer, the way your home looks—then do something about it. In the long run, you'll spend much more time letting it bother you than it would take to eliminate the clutter.

One Area at a Time

Pick one area of your house. Start in your front hall or den or a closet. If that seems too much for one day, then focus on a tabletop. Pick up each object and ask yourself if you use it. If you do, then choose a place to store the item and move on to the next. If it's a decorative item, ask yourself if it reflects your goals and vision of the future. If it doesn't, then throw it away.

Don't be distracted by other areas of the room. And don't make a pile of objects to decide where they'll go later. Actually remove each object and put it in its permanent place or in the trash, so it can be taken away when you're done. A good deal of you clutter consists of objects that are perpetually being moved from one place to another.

Do one area or piece of furniture a day, and in a couple weeks, you'll have plowed through a whole houseful of clutter. You'll also be able to see the tangible results of your efforts, and it won't take long hours to get it all done.

Alternatives to Throwing Away Clutter

Aside from the often unworkable practice of regiving gifts, you can often turn unusable gifts or unneeded objects into something else. A cookie jar can become a nail holder, a large vase, an umbrella stand. Use your throwaway clothes as cleaning rags, and your old welcome mat as a dog bed. If you like to make candles, use an old pot to melt wax and store it with your craft supplies. But don't keep an old pot on the off chance you will want to make candles sometime in the future.

If you can't bear to throw the object out, lend it to someone else. You get the best of both worlds—you are recycling, yet you're not giving the object up for good. In fact, you'll probably forget your friend has the object, because you never really needed it.

A final word: Don't become compulsive about eliminating your clutter. The goal is to clear your life up enough so that clutter is no longer a problem you have to spend time or thought on. If you're agonizing over the fact that you've cleared out your closets but your back yard still looks like a junk sale—relax. You've accomplished something wonderful already. Wait until satisfaction seeps into you before pressing on.

11 | *Collectors*

Are you the type of person who saves all the newspapers and magazines you receive, moving them from your coffee table, to under the table, then into closets? Perhaps you eventually cut or tear out some articles and put them into files, while the bulk of the periodicals lie in piles around the house. When these piles start spilling from beneath your desk and out of every corner, you know you have a problem with information collecting.

Many people collect knickknacks: thimbles, plates, owls, unicorns.... You receive them as gifts or buy them yourself. Knickknack collecting can be an interesting and fun way to channel your collecting instincts, but when your group of glassblown figurines grows to a shelf, then onto bookcases jumbled in among other collections of knickknacks, you have a problem with knickknack collecting.

Then, there are those people who will collect anything: objects they find on the street, objects their friends and neighbors are getting rid of, even objects their spouse tries to throw or give away. These people don't necessarily go out and buy more objects, but odd bits and pieces seem to gravitate to them. Do you build sheds and install shelves or cabinets to house these things you think will come in handy? The junk collecting habit is the most harmful, simply because there is a never ending source of throwaway objects just waiting to be picked up.

With all of these collecting habits, the most important consideration is your time. When your collecting habit takes up more time than the objects are worth, then your collecting has gotten out of control. A little can be a wonderful thing—overabundance is clutter. The key to eliminating useless clutter is to evaluate the items you collect.

Information Collecting

When in doubt, throw resource information away. You can find those same magazines or newspapers in your local library whenever you need them. The articles are cataloged according to subject and author in the library—easy to find and copy.

Don't keep articles simply because you read them and found them interesting. You'll read many interesting articles during your life. If you don't need the information for a certain project you have in mind, then don't keep the article. Besides, most magazines are cyclical with their articles. You'll likely see the same subject covered again.

If you feel you must keep a record of these articles, write down the name of the periodical, the title of the article, and the author. File it where you will need it most. Form an Interesting Articles File if that's the type of article you keep wanting to save. Note how often you go to this file to refer to the list of articles. It won't be often, just as it's not often you read those old periodicals.

Do you have old comics you've been saving for forty years, waiting for a time when they will be valuable? Or when your grandchildren can read them? If you have boxes of periodicals *waiting* for action, then take action. Find out if those magazines are worth anything. Give the comics to your grandchildren. Don't save periodicals when they aren't being regularly read or used by the family.

Information clutterers are lucky. You don't have any decisions to make or sorting to do. All you have to do is throw out your piles of periodicals and stacks of clipped articles. Keep reminding yourself that it's a waste of space, it's unsightly, and piles collect dust. If you consistently save newspapers and magazines, you can cure yourself of this habit now by throwing them all away.

Remember—you can always get hold of this information more quickly and easily than if you let your periodicals pile up in unwieldy stacks.

Knickknack Collecting

When dust clings to every surface because of the overabundance of knickknacks, then it's time to make a change.

Often certain types of knickknacks become a personal sign of the collector—you could not imagine living without your collection. To overcome your reluctance to part with a collection, think of when you were a child. You had many things that you adored and couldn't imagine giving up, but eventually you did give them up. You don't still have all your old toys (at least, I hope not!) because an adult helped you decide when you should get rid of them.

Become your own adult figure, and decide for yourself that you will no longer be burdened with an overabundance of knickknacks scattered throughout your house. Are you afraid that you'll miss them and hate yourself for throwing them away? Then wrap them up and store them in a box. All of them.

Get used to the knickknacks being gone from your sight. After a few months, or even a year, go through the box and you will see how little you missed those knickknacks. Oh, you'll remember them when you see them, but notice how often you exclaim, "I forgot about this one!" or "Now I remember this one!" You forgot you had these knickknacks, yet your life was not deprived in any way by their disappearance.

After storing the knickknacks for some time, try giving

them away. Or selling them. Or simply throw them away. You may decide to keep a few that suit the environment you're trying to create, but the decision will be easier because your feelings will be more defined after not seeing the knickknacks for a while.

Getting rid of your possessions can be hard at first. You invest so much of your care and time on your knickknacks and have identified yourself with them for so long. But you are faced with a unique opportunity—to change your life for the better. You can truly become someone new when your old habits and associations are gone. You can look to the future, rather than huddling over your things to reassure you of who you are. Wouldn't you prefer that?

Junk Collecting

You walk a fine line when you salvage junk. If you always need wood, by all means, salvage what wood you find. Recycling is the wave of the future, and it's good to reuse objects instead of introducing new items into the world.

But when your wood pile looms as tall as you are, then it's time to reconsider the wisdom of salvaging more wood. You obviously don't use as much as you thought you did. When you begin to salvage on the premise that "I might need this some day" you're on the wrong track.

Beware of these phrases: "I know someone who could use this," "This is practically new," "This could come in handy." All of these thoughts imply that the object is not wanted now but may be wanted in the future. *Always* throw away objects you're saving because you might need them in the future—it's a sure sign of clutter. If you have piles of junk that are waiting to be useful, then start throwing things away and stop picking up clutter.

12 | *Storage*

Do you find yourself tossing objects in the first handy place when you want them out of sight? Is every nook and corner filled with odds and ends? Do you have trouble finding things or feel as if you don't know what's in your own home?

Most of your possessions are stored in some manner until it's time to use them. Unless your possessions are organized in a way that makes them easy to find and use, then they are clutter.

Where

When deciding where an object should be kept, there are two important rules to remember:

1. How often is the object used? Store it high or conveniently low accordingly.
2. Where is the object used? Store it in a place convenient to where you use the object.

The more frequently you use an object, the more accessible it should be. Ideally, all frequently used objects should be stored in the handiest areas on reachable shelves, in cabinets, and in drawers.

Also, keep similar objects together. Put all office supplies in one drawer, all underwear in another. Sounds fairly simple, doesn't it? Well, what about your junk drawer...the one that holds various bits of often used stuff—from office supplies to champagne corks, from matches to hair ribbons? That's clutter.

At some point, you'll find objects that have no clearly defined category and no relation to other miscellaneous objects. Don't simply store these objects in the first handy space; it will defeat your purpose of organization. You will never remember where everything is.

Consider the use of each object. Binoculars are used outside the house, so a closet or shelf near the door most frequently used is the best solution. If you vacuum your living room more often than your bedroom, put the vacuum in the closet nearest to the living room rather than in the garage. If you exercise in the den, then store the equipment there.

Objects that aren't used as often (small things like maps, resource books, candles, a magnifying glass) should have their own storage places as well. But these don't have to be as easily accessible as the small useful items you frequently use.

Your larger possessions that you don't often use—perhaps your sewing machine, typewriter, electric blanket, and fan—can be stored safely but not necessarily at your fingertips. Try to keep these things together in one closet or cupboard. You'll find yourself automatically turning to that place when you think of a useful object you don't use often. If you scatter these possessions among your active objects, they start to look like clutter.

Odds and Ends

Small stuff that slides under the sofa cushions; objects that fill junk drawers because there's no other place for them; keys, matches, candles, flashlights, loose change; these things belong in storage containers or racks.

Have a certain drawer or shelf where these objects go, with individual containers for each type of supply or object. Then, if you come across a small piece of clutter, you can return it to its proper place.

Matches, candles, and flashlights are really the same thing, so store them in the same drawer. That way you know exactly where they are in case of a power outage.

Collect your loose change in one place. Store the loose change in the place where you most often pull it out of your pocket or purse. If it's when you take off your clothes at night, put a caddy in your bathroom or bedroom. If it's when you clean out your purse, put a basket or dish in your office area. If it's after grocery shopping, put jar in the kitchen. That saves you the step of transferring it to its proper place.

Always mark keys for their use: back door, front door, shed, country house, gate, etc. Keep the key in the lock or padlocks when they're not in use. It's usually best if you hang your keys. When you put them in a basket, the useless keys can remain for the rest of your life, especially if they aren't marked.

A key holder with each hook marked is the best alternative to a basket or jar. It can be placed beside a door for easy access and low enough for responsible children to reach.

If you always come in the front door, but the other keys are stored at the back door, put a hook or basket by the front door for your car and house keys. This will eliminate the constant problem of losing your keys.

Objects that people usually think are odds and ends can often be stored with other, similar objects. Shoe polish, sunglasses, and lint brush are clothing accessories. Coasters and ashtrays can be stored in the same place as your place mats and tablecloths, or in a drawer in the living room where they will be used. Scratch paper can be stored by the phone and near the door for messages. Safety pins are bathroom accessories, as are Band-Aids, hair ties, and sunscreen. Small toys should be kept in a box with larger toys, not scattered throughout the house.

Closets

Make certain each closet is organized to best suit your needs. What will you be storing in the closet? Books, games, linen, supplies? Does the closet have shelves? Are they spaced to make maximum use of the closet? Is the closet in a useful area of the house for its storage purpose?

If you're storing children's games, they need to be handy to the child so you won't have to remove them. If it's linen, use the closet nearest the laundry. The pantry should be next to the kitchen. Assess your house and if necessary, reassign closets to better suit your needs. A closet between the living room and kitchen that is currently filled with photographic equipment, albums, assorted boxes, or luggage, could be reassigned to hold kitchen overflow, such as spare china, tablecloths, and TV trays.

How you store your possessions depends on how often you use them. Clear plastic bins are best for objects you need to get to regularly. Jars and open baskets are another alternative to let you see what you have. Keep these storage containers on the most handy shelves.

When storing your possessions for a long time, boxes are the easiest method. Be sure to label the box clearly on several sides.

If there's no light in the closet, store a flashlight on one of the handy shelves. Or you can sink a hook in the ceiling and attach the flashlight to a long string. You can tie a slip knot to dangle the flashlight over your head as a light or leave the string free to hold the flashlight in your hand for corner searching.

Cleaning Out Closets

Choose one closet to start on and decide what it might best be used for. Have some boxes handy for throw away as well as for storage.

If you've decided that the hall closet will hold general family storage, such as tools, equipment, photo albums, and games, you can begin organizing that closet, removing all kitchen, bedroom, and clothing storage—or assigning separate shelves to each category.

When reorganizing a closet, don't pull everything out at once and pile it around you. Work on one shelf at a time.

Pick up each object and ask yourself if you've used this in the past year. The past two years? Ever? What are you holding onto it for? Does it have sentimental meaning for you?

If you can't pinpoint the usefulness or your special attachment to the object, ask yourself if it might come in handy someday. If the answer is yes—get rid of it. Throw the object out or give it away. It's clutter if it doesn't have a purpose right now in your life.

Some objects that are specific mementos will be boxed for semipermanent storage. Go through these boxes once a year or every couple of years. Make it a point to ELIMINATE the least important items.

Then redistribute useful objects to their proper places. Papers go in the office area, books in the bookshelves, clothes in your clothes closet. It might help to have several boxes as catchalls, to semi-sort the objects you pull from the closet until they can be stored in their proper place.

If you want the object to be returned to the closet you are working on, put it aside or in the appropriate box. Once you've cleared the unused and out-of-place items, you can begin arranging the closet you are working on.

Frequently used items are best stored on low and middle shelves, and less often used items on top shelves or in the back and corners of the closet. Keep items used at the same time together—such as bowling ball, bag, and shoes or projector and slides. Never stack more than three items on top of one another.

Creating New Storage Space

Often a clutter problem is really a space problem. You don't have room for everything, so it all becomes jumbled together and things become difficult to find. Then you can't use your possessions as you would like to because they aren't easily accessible.

Always organize existing space before trying to add new furniture or shelves. Never buy a new filing cabinet or dresser or install new shelves unless you've gone through everything in the old storage space and thrown out as much as you can. If you don't do that, eventually you'll have rooms of concealed clutter.

If you simply don't have room, then it's time to add space.

A Warning: Keep an eye out for small spaces, such as the area between your couch and sofa, or a bare wall in your bathroom. Whatever you do, don't fill every niche. The beauty of getting rid of clutter is discovering and cherishing those small spaces. Think of them as the frames in your house, setting off a grouping of furniture or balancing a room. When searching for new space, always keep the frames in mind.

Think creatively. You don't want to get out the electric screwdriver until it's absolutely necessary. Shelves can be used to store items other than books. With small clutter, it's best to place the items in baskets or boxes so that the shelf still looks attractive. Or, you can hang an interesting drape over the lower shelves to hide the storage behind it. Store larger objects, such as typewriters, fans, and sleeping bags on the bottom and top shelves of large bookcases.

Toy boxes can be used as general game holders for adults, too. Or your antique hope chest can be filled with linen or clothing. If your files only fill one file drawer, use the other to store supplies.

Use screens and curtained corners and niches to hide loaded shelves or a full area of your house. This way you turn an eyesore into a decorative asset. In a similar way, you can place tall bookcases so that they jut out, creating a niche in a large room. A desk or table can be placed inside this new alcove for added privacy. This is particularly useful for wide bookcases which allow for storage from both sides.

Objects designed for organizing your clutter usually don't work as well as you'd like. But in a few essential areas, you can get a lot of use out of them. For the shower: hooks or trays to hold soap, washcloth, comb, shampoo, conditioner, shaving cream, and razor; boxes (such as a sewing box) or traveling kits for makeup or hair articles. Small and large containers and racks to organize your odds and ends are almost essential.

Shelves
The best place to build shelves is in a closet. Then you don't have to worry about unsightly items in plain view. In large closets, line one side with shelves. This is especially good for children. One side can be used for clothes and the other for toys.

In shallow closets, there is the danger of the shelves being too deep if you shelve in the entire space. Perhaps the bottom shelf could be the width of the closet, but the others should be narrower. Otherwise, your possessions will disappear into the dark recesses never to be seen again. Always remember: You are building shelves to make things handy, not hide them away.

If you don't want to go to the trouble of building shelves, simply place a large chest of drawers in the closet. This doesn't use all the available space, but it is an easy solution.

In small rooms, especially laundry, pantry, or furnace rooms, build shelves supported by floor-to-ceiling posts. This dramatically increases the use of those rooms, which are intended to store quantities of objects.

If possible, install adjustable shelves. Then store items of the same size on the same shelves. You can also add more shelves later if needed.

In bedrooms, a shelf just below the ceiling all around the room is a decorative way to store items not used frequently. In children's rooms, stuffed animals, dolls, or figurines may be displayed; in other rooms, books, photo albums, and mementos. A good way to retrieve these items is by using an expandable pincher claw. Everyone should have a tool such as this, or similar, to retrieve small items that have fallen behind or under the heavy furniture.

Plants may either be hung or shelved. Try to keep plants off the tops of tables. Good places for shelves may be a corner near a window, within the window frame itself, or under the window. Plants can also be hung from a ceiling hook with a butterfly bolt or from a triangle hinge attached to the wall.

Hanging Items

Hooks placed on the backs of doors are the most convenient method of hanging. You use space that is currently going to waste while keeping the hanging objects out of sight. Nightgowns, pajamas, and bathrobes can be hung on the back of the bathroom door, outdoor clothing on the back of a hall closet hear the door, shoes in a hanging shoe tree, or ties on multiple hangers hung on a hook on the back of your closet door. Be inventive. Anything that you often use is a good possibility for hanging on the back of a door.

If you don't have enough door space, hang hooks along the back of the closet for your camera, binoculars, extra purses, and bags. Anything with a shoulder strap can be stored by hanging it up.

If your space is very limited, consider hanging possessions from the ceiling or high on the wall. This can include: exercise equipment, bicycles, folding chairs, TV trays, musical instruments, etc. Large pegs will serve to remove these objects from your way while making them easy to reach.

New Possessions

When you buy something new, immediately decide where its permanent storage place will be. Don't assume it will fall into the right place automatically—that will ensure the item sits around indefinitely until you get tired of looking at it.

When you decide right away, you might eventually have to move the object to a new place that's more convenient, but at least the new possession never becomes clutter. It will also keep you from acquiring useless objects if you always associate a place for the object with the object. If you don't know how a new object will fit into your house, it's time to reevaluate your need for it.

13 | *Household Clutterers*

If clutter is a common household problem, then everyone living in your home, whether it's a roommate, spouse, child or other member of your family, must acknowledge that clutter is a problem. If you have trouble getting others to pay attention and take this problem seriously, then ask everyone to admit out loud that the household has a clutter problem.

Discuss what sort of environment each individual envisions for the household. If there are different expectations, someone is going to end up unhappy with the effort. Decide before you start what your collective goals are; knowing these will motivate you. Then, everyone else involved needs to acknowledge responsibility to take part in trying to make changes.

Set a specified length of time, let's say a week to start with, and get a commitment from each person to leave a room in better shape when left than when entered. That means restacking the magazines on the coffee table, or throwing out a magazine no longer wanted, or taking a glass into the kitchen, or sorting through an old pile of stuff piled on the piano. It doesn't have to be a huge effort, because if everyone follows this rule, your house will gradually become clutter-free. It will also help you pinpoint the trouble spots—particular members of your family or rooms that have a clutter problem.

Spouses and Clutter

Compromise is in order when one or both partners are clutterers. Usually each person has a special clutter problem—for example, the husband may be a collector while the wife can't organize her time.

First, each must respect the other's right to choose how to live. But each also has the right not to be inconvenienced by the other. These two principles must be kept in balance. One person's habits or preference should not be allowed to disrupt the household or prevent a spouse from living "normally."

Usually, each person needs to have a private space, be it a desk or a room, of his or her own. Make the private spaces as equal as possible, otherwise tensions will arise. If you have one extra room, divide it with bookshelves, or temporary screens, or build a partition. Hobbies and work should be done in the private space rather in the general areas. Both can agree not to clutter the dining room table (mutual space), while clutter is allowed in your own room or desk if you want.

Depending on the size of your house, each spouse may have more than one private area. Discuss this and determine which areas belong to whom. Designate the remainder of the house as general-use areas. The general-use areas should always be cleaned of your clutter after you use it, unlike your private area, which may be left semicluttered if you are in the middle of a project.

If your spouse claims ignorance as the reason for any sort of clutter—clothes, paper work, dishes, or cleaning, then take the time to demonstrate exactly how the task is done or where the objects go.

All it takes is developing new habits, but if your spouse consistently "forgets," there is something more going on. Perhaps your spouse doesn't understand the overall goal you both are striving toward. Perhaps there are personal insecurities or preoccupations involved, and this is the clearest (even if it is subconscious) signal for help and attention. Don't look at clutter problems as something negative: This issue is a way to open up communication between the two of you so you can learn more about each other.

Set a good example for everyone in your household. It will become increasingly clear who hasn't developed a clear vision of the desired environment. Then you have the opportunity to help your spouse move forward.

Cleaning

Set one day or a couple evenings aside when both partners will do the general cleaning. You can either rotate chores or do the same tasks every week. This schedule needn't be ironclad: If one person misses a cleaning night, he can do his set tasks the next day. Sit down and talk it out. Perhaps you hate to do the dishes, but you don't mind making the bed and straightening the bedroom.

Both should be conscientious in performing tasks. Men, even today, do less than ten minutes of housework a week, while women do eighty minutes. Try to equalize this statistic in your home. If you're moving toward a common future, your environment is mutually important.

If nothing works, then stop picking up after your spouse. Let the laundered clothes lie in piles around the bedroom, let the dishes lie in the sink. Point out what you are doing and explain exactly why you are doing it. Keep in mind that you want to open up communication, not fight him into doing what you want. When you're married and working toward a common future, the problem belongs to both, not just one of you.

When you discuss your clutter problems, you'll find most negligence problems come under the concept of "fair exchange." For example, he says he picked up the laundry on the way home and he worked late anyway to make more money, so he doesn't have to clean the bathroom. You're remembering that you dropped off the laundry and now you know you will have to put it away, so why can't he clean the bathroom? This all usually goes on without communication, so neither one knows how much the other has really done.

Communication is the key. Keeping your physical space in order and progressing toward the future you want is as important as any aspect of your lives. Talk about it thoroughly and supportively, being honest with yourself and your spouse about motivations and desires.

Children and Clutter

You don't want to nag or pick up after your children, so what are the alternatives? Children can be taught organizational skills, and the younger they start, the better prepared they will be for the rest of their lives.

Make putting things away as easy as possible to encourage them to participate. An adjustable tension rod is a handy way to make hanging clothes easy for children to reach. It can be adjusted as the children get older. The hamper should stay in the closet or bedroom where the child normally gets undressed. Make supplies accessible, so there's no difficulty about getting them or putting them away.

Toy Storage
If your children always play in the basement, put the toy storage there, even if the basement is used as a family den. A pretty wooden box is an alternative better than having stuffed animals and action dolls scattered across the floor. If your children routinely throw their toys in a particular area

(or clothes for that matter), put the toy box (or hamper) there. Then you don't have to fight their old habits to get them to clean up their clutter.

If the majority of your children's play will take place in the bedroom, arrange a corner for toy and game storage as well as creative supplies. Buy a table and chair that are comfortable for the children. Allow them to keep special projects out on their table or in a particular corner of the room (to set up a doll house or racetrack).

One large storage box is not necessarily the best alternative—the toys become jumbled and difficult to find. Low shelves, stackable bins, drawers, or several boxes are good ways to organize toys. Keep small toys and games in boxes, bins, or baskets. Mark the outside of the containers with a picture of the toy or a colored label (if the child is old enough to read) so that the contents are clear.

When your child gets a new game or toy, help her decide where its storage place will be. Don't make the decision for her, that will ensure she won't learn how to do it for herself. Besides, it is her room, and children ought have a say in where their possessions go.

Cleaning

Set clear standards for cleaning. Does the blanket have to be folded every day, or the sheets smoothed and tucked? Can the toy cars be put with the soldiers, or can all the craft supplies be jumbled together in one box? When does the entire room have to be cleared of clutter, with toys and games put in their proper places? Is it once a day, every couple of days, or once a week?

When it comes time to clean the room, prompt your child to see the scattered toys and clothing as objects that have their proper place. Ask them to fetch all the big toys or stuffed animals first and put them in their place. Then gather the smaller toys together. Then the creative supplies.

Then the clothes. This categorizes the objects in the child's mind and avoids forcing him to do the more daunting task of working systematically from door to bed.

Keep the cleaning tasks suited to the child's age. When a child is very young, work together in the cleaning. While the child picks up the blocks, you gather the stuffed animals. As the child gets older, his responsibilities should increase.

Make a game of the cleaning, or tell a story while you work. This will create good associations in the child's mind with clearing clutter from his room.

The best way to teach your child how to keep clutter from invading the household is by example. Both parents benefit by keeping the house clean together, and the children should be included as much as possible in the process.

Getting Rid of Children's Clutter

Helping a child learn when it is time to get rid of unused or old possessions is the best thing you can do to prevent another clutter collector from entering the world. Approach clutter elimination with the attitude that "things" are in a constant motion. Possessions come into your life and at some point they leave it.

If a child resists throwing or giving something away, never force her. Explain your own system of putting objects aside when you aren't sure so that you can decide over time whether you want to keep that possession or not. Set a shelf or space aside in the child's room where she can see these objects. Let her make the final decision whether she wants to keep the object or get rid of it.

Children are allowed to be pack rats more than adults because their possessions become invested with meaning that parents may not know about or understand. Don't create a lifetime pack rat by being too obsessive about your child's throwing away his belongings. As children grow up, they will naturally discard things they are "too old" to play with. If not, discuss the child's feelings about the toy or object and maybe you'll get insight into what motivates your child. Don't just try to force a child into the mold you see as "right."

If your child has many toys and games that aren't often played with, store them for a few months and then bring them out again. It will add novelty to the toys; and if the child still doesn't play with them, then it's time to suggest getting rid of these toys. If the child hesitates, put the toy in the think-about-it area.

Adolescents and Clutter

Hopefully, by the time your children grow into adolescence, you will have instilled proper clutter-consciousness in them so that you don't have to battle over messy rooms. If an adolescent perennially keeps his room a mess, then the cause may be something other than a lack of organization or cleanliness.

It's not a good idea to clean an adolescent's room for him. He will never be faced with the results of his lack of effort if you do it for him. Besides, most adolescents don't want their parents in their rooms, or drawers, or closets. Parents need to respect the right to privacy as part of growing up and moving out from under the protective parental umbrella.

Also, adolescents don't want to be told what to do about themselves or their possessions. Their physical and emotional privacy is of utmost importance. If you can stand it, simply tell your children to keep their doors closed until they outgrow their messiness.

But, or course, your best course of action is to talk about it with your child. Again, don't try to tell her what you think she should be doing. Make sure she understands the idea of envisioning her future and then working with her environment so that it reflects that future. Keep in mind that it's more difficult with adolescents because they don't have the control over their environment that you do—the house reflects the idea of your future, not theirs. That's why it's important to respect your children's space, because, messy or not, it's the physical arena where they can experiment with what they want in their lives.

14 | *Household Clutter*

An efficient and well-kept house is an impossible dream, right? Wrong. Only two things need to be considered when you want to bring order to your house: a place for everything that you use and everyone putting things back in place.

Except for rare exceptions, it's best to confine activities to one area only. Remember that objects become clutter when unlike things are mumbled together. In the interest of finding items easily and not maintaining unnecessary duplicates, keep similar objects and activities together.

Living Room

The living room or den has the most potential for becoming cluttered. Objects naturally gravitate to the living room because it is the center of the household. Don't attempt to keep your family's possessions out of the living room—that will simply render it useless.

Do consider whether every activity that goes on in the living room should continue to be done there. Perhaps it would be better if you kept your sewing in your bedroom or workroom. Exercise space could also be switched. Hobbies should be confined to one area and provided with adequate storage space. If the living room is often noisy, then put the phone in a different room, such as the foyer, the breakfast nook, or under the stairs.

66

If your house has both a den and a living room, assign certain activities to each. You could keep one room particularly clean for entertaining, while the other retains a more casual atmosphere where snacks and games-in-progress are permitted.

The Cleaning Process

Start small. Consider one corner first, or one unit of furniture at a time (sofa, coffee table, and end table). Consider each object, including furniture, and determine if it truly belongs in the living room.

Your possessions should be stored near the area where they are used. Don't store old magazines and newspapers in the living room—throw them away. But you can store a heating pad in an end table if you always use it while sitting on the sofa.

Gather similar objects and store them in the same area. Don't fill empty niches with miscellaneous objects—that translates into clutter. Stored along with the heating pad could be your sewing box (if you sew in the living room), reading glasses, books waiting to be read—whatever else you do while seated on the couch. Coasters, ashtrays, and matches could be in one drawer. TV trays, folding chairs, and card table naturally go together. Liquor, glasses, ice bucket, tongs, and corkscrew should be in one cabinet.

Often, one multipurpose wall unit with cabinets and shelves is the best way to take care of organizing your living room. Or you can use a large sideboard with divided drawers and shelves to store your possessions.

Workroom

The workroom is the best place for multiple activities. With a large work surface, you can set up space and storage for each hobby or activity. Additional surfaces can be set up for semipermanent activities: building models, jig-saw puzzles, ironing board for sewing, typewriter table, etc. Get tables that are the right height for working, either standing or sitting.

Store the items used on each work surface nearby, either in a drawer or on a shelf. Shelves above or to one side of the work surface serve as excellent active storage. Buy plastic bins or baskets to hold your project supplies and to keep them from mixing with supplies for other projects.

A pegboard over the main work area is a good place to hang your supplies and tools. They are visible and within easy reach. If you like, outline the tool or label the peg to remind you where everything goes. You will be able to see more clearly which tools and supplies you use and which are outmoded or unnecessary. Get rid of any items you never use.

Be sure to clean off the main work surface after you are done for the day, especially if you're not certain which project you will be working on next.

Kitchen

To eliminate clutter in your kitchen, store things in the most logical and convenient places. If you put the frequently used items in the handiest places, kitchen clutter will be easy to spot. Store your glasses in the cupboard by the refrigerator, put the coffee mugs on the shelf over the coffee machine, hang the pot holders beside the oven.

Keep similar items together on each shelf, but don't necessarily keep all the drinking utensils in one cabinet, all the plates in another, and so on. It is more useful to store items that are used together in the same place, such as baking utensils. The rolling pin, bowl, and sifter can all go on the same shelf or drawer.

China and service ware of the same pattern needn't be

stored together, either. If you have six people in your family, put six of each pattern on a handy shelf. The others can be stored on a less accessible shelf.

Duplication

Go through each drawer and shelf. If you have unnecessary duplication, like several can openers or four knife sharpeners, keep only one or, at most, two. Give the others away or throw them out. If you haven't used your eggbeater in two years, toss it out. When you need one, you can buy another. If you have lots of space, group your utensils in two drawers, those you often use and those you only use when doing the holiday baking.

The same can be said of plates, glasses, and pots and pans. Five frying pans and no space for your new pressure cooker? Throw out a few frying pans. Twenty-four shot glasses and no space for your tea glasses? Give most of those shot glasses to a friend who likes to have parties.

Appliances and Accessories

If you use canisters, keep them all in one area. If you don't use canisters, they are clutter and you can get rid of them.

If you don't have much counter space, get rid of that bulky knife block. You can store your knives in a drawer organizer or in a handy organizer that attaches to the bottom of one of your cabinets. It folds out of sight and keeps your knives from being jumbled together in a drawer.

A spinning tray can revive a uselessly deep corner cabinet. Put your spices on it, or canisters, or utensil jugs.

Put away all appliances that aren't used daily. If your toaster oven is only used on Sundays, assign it to a suitably handy shelf or drawer. The same goes for cookbooks.

Spice racks are good; they limit the amount of space your spices can take up, thereby ensuring you will monitor which spices are used and which are not. Alphabetize your spices. This will take a small amount of effort to do, and the result will be an organized rack with every kind of spice easy to find.

A basket is good for holding fruit. It makes a colorful revolving display and puts the fruit where everyone is prompted to eat it.

Your refrigerator is a prime clutter collector. Organize the shelves and you will eliminate the pockets where food collects. Store frequently eaten items on the most accessible space, but remember to group similar foods together. Choose a prominent place for leftovers so that you can see them before they spoil. Date and label all wrapped leftovers that go into the freezer.

Don't leave your ironing board up. If that's a habit you can't break, invest in an ironing board that attaches to the back of a door in your kitchen or pantry. They are easy to install, and you will always flip the board up when you're done if only to be able to close the door. No more problem!

Bedroom

The best place to put frequently used items is on a handy shelf (for books or knitting), or a bedside table with a drawer (for flashlight, pad of paper, pen, extra pair of reading glasses, or cards). A strategically placed table or shelf is also handy if you plan to snack in bed. These surfaces should only be used for frequently used items, not as long- or mid-term storage. Clear anything out of this area if you don't use it at least a couple times a week.

If you have space to set up a reading area, a desk, or exercise area in your bedroom, define the area and keep only those things that pertain to the activity in this spot. If you always undress in one area, designate that as the clothes catchall with a basket or hamper, rather than letting dirty clothing spread around the room.

Under the bed is a good place for long-term storage, but beware of this habit. As with boxed storage (see *Storage*), it's best to go through everything you keep under your bed at least once a year to eliminate what you never use.

Because storage places under your bed are more accessible than the back of a closet or your basement or attic, don't use it for the long term storage. Instead, put things there you will need to get to within some months, such as off-season clothing or luggage.

Bathroom

Bathrooms offer limited options for organization. That's why manufactured organizers work best in the bathroom. The shower should have trays for shampoo, washcloth, comb, razor, and shaving cream. Makeup can be kept in one container or on one shelf.

The bathroom collects clutter faster than any room in the house. Health and beauty aids that are half used, never used, rarely used, old and empty, probably fill your bathroom storage space. Eliminate everything that you aren't using anymore. Be ruthless; these aren't possessions that you are getting rid of but packaged goods that can be bought anywhere, anytime, for little money.

Assess the storage capacity of your bathroom. Then, according to how many people will be using the bathroom, designate areas for each person's private storage. Also designate areas that are for general storage.

Follow the usual rule: Keep items that are similar together. First-aid items, such as Band-Aids, aspirin, and antiseptic, should go on one shelf or in one box clearly marked as "First Aid" and placed in general storage.

Grooming items, such as deodorant, lotion, and tweezers, can be grouped together in each person's private storage. If you have a large quantity of makeup, sort it into small baskets or boxes and put it in your private storage. If there is one large makeup box, find an appropriate place for it under the sink or on a larger shelf.

Everything for the shower should be kept in the shower. Towels and washcloths should be kept handily together under the sink or in a small dresser inside the bathroom, not in the linen closet. Toilet paper, feminine hygiene products, and paper cups could also be kept under the sink, while the cleansing products can be placed in a container on a shelf or under the sink.

Medicine Cabinet

How many bottles of old pills do you have in your medicine cabinet? How many packages of cold tablets with only three or four pills left in the foil-backed holders? Most people collect medicine inadvertently, but this can be a dangerous habit. Expiration dates pass, labels wear out or crumple off, and assorted pills with no markings lurk in every corner. The least dangerous thing that can happen is that a medicine lose its effectiveness—but that isn't good for your cut or cold, is it? Or medicine can be mixed up, causing you to take pill for constipation instead of a cold. The worst that can happen is the nightmare of medicine cabinet lore—drinking external medicine or using pet antibiotics for people.

Old prescriptions should *always* be thrown away, unless one is in regular use (thyroid medicine, birth control pills, etc.). Antibiotics lose their effectiveness with time and doctors will be unable to analyze your symptoms properly if you've already begun self-treatment.

Over-the-counter medicine should also be thrown out if the expiration date has passed. If you can't find the expiration date and can't remember specifically when you bought this medicine (but know it was more than six months ago), then throw it out. Also toss away anything you're not sure of; this is the time to get rid of those anonymous pills.

Any external medicine over a few years old should usually be tossed out. Age and air can affect medicine, lessening its effectiveness.

Entryway

This should always be a general use area, and it therefore is one of your clutter-free areas. Besides, it is the first place visitors see and you want their impression to be favorable.

If objects must be stored in the entryway, be sure to have proper storage for them. A shelf in the closet can hold possessions you often use, rather than those stored over the long-term. Outdoor toys and games, binoculars, and sporting equipment are best kept in this closet. Install low hooks on the back of the door for outdoor clothing. Hooks are much easier and quicker to get to than hangers. Hats, coats, scarfs, and gloves with strings can also be hung up. Or you can string a clothesline with clothespins to hang gloves and mittens. Boots should be stored on a dripping rack on the bottom of a closet nearest the door.

A coatrack is good for older children, adults, and especially guests. Make certain the stand is on a hard surface rather than a carpet so that dripping rain and snow don't cause harm.

It's also good to have an umbrella stand. You will always have umbrellas, and this is the most convenient way to store them. Buy a conventional stand or a large decorated vase.

15 | *Clothing Clutter*

Even if you spend thousands of dollars, your attempts to compile a complete wardrobe can be easily destroyed if your useful clothes get lost among the clothing clutter.

You need to assess your wardrobe in the same way you examine your houshold environment. What do you intend to be in your future? What are you now? If you don't work full-time, why are your business suits still given priority in your closet? Be honest with yourself. If an item of clothing is not being used or contradicts the image you have of yourself, then it doesn't belong in your life.

Sorting

Examining and evaluating your clothes once a year is the best way to organize your wardrobe. Each year, you'll have the benefit of last year's efforts to build on. Eventually, it will become second nature to decide what should happen with each item of clothing, thereby eliminating the clutter.

To examine your clothes, try on everything you haven't worn in the past year. You'll be amazed at the finds you come across.

It's like finding a whole new wardrobe you didn't know existed. Get rid of clothes that don't fit and never have fit to your satisfaction. Get rid of clothes that don't flatter you. Why bother using precious space for clothing that you never wear?

To sort, you must decide if an item of clothing is:

1. useful, and needs to be hung or put in a drawer;
2. unused, and needs to be thrown away;
3 undecided, and can be put on hold for a year;
4. a specific memento, and needs to be properly stored.

Many people with seasonal wardrobes and small closets store their off-season clothes in boxes or seldom used suitcases. The yearly examination can be done in the spring or fall when it's time to shift your wardrobe from boxes to closets anyway.

Unused Clothing

The easy clothes are ones you never wear; when you try them on, you wonder what ever made you to buy a rag like that in the first place. Bag those clothes and take them to the thrift store; or turn them into rags, or have a garage sale, or give them to a friend. If your rejected clothes hang around in a bag at the bottom of your closet for another year, then give it up. Recycling is always best, but if you just can't bring yourself to do it, then throw the clothes out.

Undecided Clothing

If you're not sure you like the item of clothing, put it in a special section where you can see it when you open your closet. Then the option is always in front of your eyes. If a year rolls by and you still haven't worn that skirt or shirt or whatever, you can push it aside.

After another year, if a piece of clothing is still hanging in your closet and you haven't managed to put it on your body except during your yearly checks, throw it out.

Mementos

Evaluate how important each item of clothing is, in and of itself. Does it remind you of a particular event or a time in your life? If you have a whole rack of clothes like this, be ruthless. Pick out your favorites and keep only the unique clothing. Keep only one of the pairs of pants that proves you once fit into a size six—if you absolutely must. After all, it's not the clothes that are important, but your memories of that special trip or the prom.

These treasured pieces should be kept in a separate place. After all, you aren't wearing them anymore. They don't belong among the other clothes you wear; they now fall into the category of mementos. If you have adequate storage space, box these clothes and label the outside clearly on all four sides and the top. If you live where space is limited, you can store your "clothes treasures" in a seldom used suitcase. That way, a suitcase that's taking up space anyway has a legitimate purpose in your life.

If a year or two has gone by and you have new items you must add to the memento box, bring the box or suitcase down and get ready for a ride down memory lane. If you pull out several items that remind you of the same thing, person, or place, get rid of two and keep only one. If you can't remember where you wore it but always liked it, get rid of it. That's right. You have plenty of things that you like to wear, that you still do wear. Just because you once liked something or even treasured it doesn't mean it's right for you now.

Try to cut down on the bulk of your mementos. This is where you can practice moderation for a year or two. If you're not sure, tag an item to remind yourself about it the next time you go through the box. By then, you'll probably be a little more certain you want to get rid of it. If you're still not completely certain, tag it again. The next time you look through the box, if the item doesn't make you tingle with memories, get rid of it.

Clothes Closet

What should be kept in your clothes closet? Always keep in mind that this closet is for your clothes. That will keep other types of possessions from accumulating in that space.

Your clothing, shoes, and accessories get first priority, then boxed clothing and suitcases that can be fit in as long as there's room.

The quickest way to gather useless clothes (or clutter) is by not knowing what you have. Organizing your closet will make your wardrobe needs clear at a glance.

Hang as many clothes as possible. With the clothes in orderly rows, it makes it easier to mix and match. In organizing drawers, put the most frequently used items in the handiest places. Store your underwear and nightwear in a prime spot. Sweaters, which are worn only during part of the year, can be put in an out-of-the-way drawer, then switched with the T shirts during winter, to make the sweaters handy again.

Don't mix work clothes, play clothes, and dressy clothes. Arrange clothing so that the same type hangs together. Shirts with shirts, next to the jackets, next to the sweaters, and so on. Even if you have several favorite outfits, don't mix the skirts and shirts together in the prime space. You're cheating yourself of all the possibilities your wardrobe offers.

Don't keep clothes that are a smaller or larger size than you currently wear hanging in your closet while you wait to diet into them or have just dieted out of them. If it helps to motivate your diet by seeing these clothes, display them prominently, but not indefinitely. After a while, your eyes skim over those jeans and they no longer give you the benefit of their impact. The same sorting procedure still applies. Make the item handy, and if you haven't worn it in a year, then it's time to remove it from the active lines.

Hang clothes that need to be mended in a special place in your closet. Storing these clothes in drawers is not a good idea because that puts the items out of sight (therefore out of mind). If the clothes are in front of your eyes, yet you know you can't wear them, then the incentive to mend them will be greater.

If you're like most people, you take off your clothes at night and toss them somewhere. If you've been doing this all your life, don't expect to be able to mend this habit quickly. *Pick one place* as your toss pile. It can be one chair in your room or the top of the laundry hamper. This is the pile that is waiting to be sorted—things that aren't dirty should be hung up, preferably inside out so you'll remember it's already been worn once. The dirty clothes then to into the hamper or laundry bag.

Accessories

Organize your accessories in an accessible space where they are visible. If you have extra drawers, divide one into compartments or lay the belts and scarves flat, like a fan of cards, so that the edge of all the items are visible.

If you have shelf space, put the accessories in open-ended boxes so you can see what you have. You could also put accessories in the type of shoe trees with pockets that hang on the back of a door, or arrange them on a multiple hanger. If you can see what you have, you can see what you don't use. That's the first step in getting rid of clutter—knowing what you don't use.

Small accessories should have their own "toss place" on a certain area of your dresser or a small table in your bathroom. You must keep in mind, however, that these are places of transition and therefore prime clutter collectors. Accessories don't belong permanently in the "toss place," so you have to clean it off every once in a while and put jewelry and hair ribbons back where they belong.

Shoes

Buy a shoe tree. It keeps your active shoes from forming a clutterlike pile on the bottom of your closet. It also keeps your shoes in good shape and displays them for easy access. Most shoe trees hang on the inside of your closet door, so they don't take up needed room. Others are stacks of boxes that can hang from your tension rod or sit directly on the floor.

Follow the same yearly examination and sorting procedure with your shoes as you do with your clothing. Try every pair on at least once a year. Put the "maybe's" in a prominent place, within easy reach. If you still don't wear those shoes, then it's time to get rid of them.

If they have special meaning to you, they belong in the memento box (your first pair of running shoes or the shoes you wore at your wedding, say). You could store these shoes with your memento clothes. If you're like most people, you won't have too many special "just for the memories" shoes. You could also store these shoes in the most inaccessible part of your shoe tree.

Buying Clothes

A good way to eliminate clutter from your wardrobe is to plot out what you have and what you need before you go shopping. Otherwise, you'll buy things aimlessly, without a plan in mind, and that leads to clutter.

Take a serious look through your wardrobe. Identify the staples of your casual and work wear. Keep these clothes in mind when you go shopping. Don't duplicate them—that's clutter—but try to buy items that will go with your most used clothing.

Coordination is one key to success with your wardrobe. If you wear browns and beiges, don't buy a shocking pink shirt no matter how much you're attracted to the bright color. The shirt will wear out its appeal and become clutter in your closet. Remember all those fluorescent clothes? The hot-pants craze? How often do you wear those clothes now?

Always consult your vision of yourself in the future to guide you in buying new clothing. If you see yourself living in the country, then buy clothing that reflects that. If you see yourself as career oriented, spend the majority of your clothing allowance on creating the sort of image you hope to project. Mostly, let your future guide your clothing choices, not your past.

16 | *Books, Records and Video Clutter*

Your book shelves don't have to be cluttered. Books, records, and video tapes are easy to organize, and once you've created a system you won't have to deal with piles or not being able to find anything.

Books

Most people don't think of clutter in their bookshelves, but it's there. Organizing your library can be a big task. Don't rush and don't worry if you have to leave boxes or piles of books around your house for a few days. The end result will be worth it.

Different techniques apply to sorting books than those used with typical clutter. You don't necessarily throw away a book that you haven't looked at in one or two years. Instead, your bookshelves need to be organized so that you don't lose sight of the fine options you have in your library (whether it's one shelf, a set of bookcases, or an entire room).

Unlike closets, don't organize each bookshelf separately. Look at all of your books before you begin. If some are boxed and waiting to be shelved, open the box and go through it to see what you have.

You will have to form categories for your library depending on the types of books you own. Assign shelf space for the books according to the frequency of use, then the size of each category.

Common Categories are:

Art
Biography
Business
Child Care
Fiction
Gardening
Health
Self Help
Reference
History
How To
Metaphysical
Psychological
Religious
Sports
Travel

Keep all reference books in one place for *easy* access. Reference books include dictionaries, encyclopedias, atlas, thesaurus, quotes, Who's Who, Farmer's Almanac®, maps, etc.

Within the larger categories, smaller categories may be made. If you own a large quantity of art books, separate them into groups by artist, period, or country. If you mostly own biographical novels, separate them into autobiography and biography, then put them in order of birth dates of the subjects or alphabetize them by name.

Fiction has many categories within it, such as:

Classics
Contemporary
Fantasy

Mystery
Romance
Science Fiction

You should also include poetry, plays, and short stories in
your Fiction category.

Shelving Books

You can either remove all books from the shelves (and
clean the shelves at the same time) or shuffle as you go
along. Block out areas for each category before you start, but
remember to be flexible. It's difficult to tell how much space
you'll need at first

Frequency of use should be the first consideration when
shelving books. The largest category of books is not necessarily the one you use the most. If you received your degree
in economics, then you may have many business books that
you no longer refer to as often as you read your fiction.

After you have decided which categories you want most
handy, categories which are similar are best grouped together rather than simply arranged alphabetically. Therefore, Health can be near "Self Help"; Metaphysical,
Psychological, and Religion should be near each other;
Biography near History; while Sports, Gardening and "How
to" can be near one another. Art and photo books are often
oversized and ought to be place near each other on more
widely spaced shelves.

Don't feel like you have to keep all your books in the same
place. If you use your many cookbooks, put a shelf in the
kitchen or pantry for easy access. Books on car maintenance
and repair can go on a shelf in the garage. Most frequently
read books (Bible, metaphysical books, your personal jour-
nal) can be put on a shelf beside your bed.

Don't cram books into the shelves. Leave space in each
category for new books that you acquire. If you own more

than one book by an author always keep those books together when shelving them.

Don't stack books on their sides; it makes removal difficult. You can double layer your books if you have no more space, but be sure to put less frequently used books in the rear and revolve them every once in a while so that you still have access to these books.

Getting Rid of Books

If you don't care enough about a book to want it on a shelf, then consider whether you want to keep that book.

If you receive a book as a gift that you never have and never will read, get rid of it. Often it happens that books that are gifts are not exactly what the recipient likes to read. Don't keep unwanted books around to clutter your shelves.

If you tried to read a book but hated it, or you bought a book and never got around to reading it, don't throw these books away yet. Keep these books together in a special section where you can get to them. Look over these books you're uncertain about over every once in a while to see if you would like to try to read one of them now. If a book sits in this section for a few years, it's time to get rid of it.

Don't toss books in the trash; recycle them along with old newspapers or give them to friends. Better yet, books can be a tax deduction you if you donate them to a library, jail, school or hospital. If you do donate them, keep a record and get a receipt.

New Shelf Space

If you need more space, here's a few options:

Free standing book cases;
plain wooden cubes that are stackable;
rows of shelves built into a wall or room divider;
single shelf where appropriate.

Records and Cassettes

You will have to form categories for your music library depending on the types of music you own. Some typical categories include:

Ballads
Classical
Country
Folk
Jazz
New Age
Show tunes
Soft and hard rock

Records and cassettes that aren't music can be categorized into:

Actors or Plays
Books on tape
Interviews
Lectures
Poetry
Self Help

Again, if you have a large category, break it into smaller sections. Classical music can be separated into opera, orchestral, vocal music, or chamber music. New Age can be split into instrumental and nature sounds.

Storing Records and Cassettes

Records can be filed in deep bookcases or cubes which have an opening in the front, or in sturdy cartons which allow access from the top. Cassette tapes are best stored in a cassette box or carrying case. If your tape collection is large, manufactured cassette containers that can be stacked or hung on the wall are a good option.

Frequency of use should be the first consideration when shelving records or cassettes. Just like books, the largest category of music is not necessarily the one you listen to the most. Before reorganizing your music library, think carefully about what you listen to. Make these categories of music the most accessible.

Within the large categories, keep the records and cassettes by the same composer or musician together, forming a subcategory. The subcategories can be arranged alphabetically. Within the subcategories, the records and cassettes can be arranged either according to date of release or alphabetically by title.

> *Examples:* Beatles records would form one subcategory within your Rock category. If you arrange the records according to release date, *Meet the Beatles* would be first, but if you arrange the records alphabetically, then *Abbey Road* would be first.

Getting Rid of Records and Cassettes

If you no longer listen to certain records or cassettes, then consider whether you want to keep them. Were these records bought when you were younger, and now you're no longer interested in them? Keep the records if you occasionally pull them out to travel down memory lane. Music is an important aid to memory; so if you hesitate strongly over a record or cassette, then don't get rid of it.

If you received the music as a gift and you never have and never will listen to it, get rid of it. If you bought a record that you don't like, and have tried to listen to it without success, then get rid of it.

You don't have to toss records or cassettes in the trash. Cassettes can be rerecorded. If you (or a friend) has the machinery to record tape-to-tape, or album-to-tape, then keep all your old cassettes. A small piece of tape over the protect hole allows you to record a whole new album that a friend has lent you, thereby saving yourself the cost of a new cassette.

If you plan on reusing old cassettes, have a special place where you can get to them quickly and where you won't be tempted to try to refile them.

If you do get rid of records and cassettes, give them to a school, hospital, or thrift shop. Like books, these are a tax deduction. Keep a record and get a receipt.

Video Tapes

Video tapes can be categorized into:

Comedy
Drama
Classic
Adventure
Television shows or series
Documentary
Exercise
Home videos
Self Help

Keep similar videos together. Arrange them consistently among the categories by date (television series) or by title (movies). Home videos can be arranged by date or by subject. All Christmas tapes can be kept together, just as all your vacation tapes can be kept together. Or simply arrange the videos according to date of taping.

Depending on the number of video tapes you own, store them on shelves or in tape boxes with sliding drawers.

Getting Rid of Video Tapes

If you no longer watch certain movies or no longer use most of your exercise tapes because you prefer one particular one, then it's time to recycle or throw away the tape.

It's usually not good to discard home videos. People tend to regret it when they do.

17 | *Office and Desk Clutter*

Is your desk crowded with objects or piles that are seldom used or referred to? You may be under the misconception that a full desk indicates a busy and competent person.

Your work environment needs to be the most efficient area of your life. Clutter is never more harmful than when it's in your office or on your desk.

Office

Use only one calendar to record appointments and deadlines, rather than recording work-related activities on one calendar and family events on another. When recording projects or events, write down all the pertinent information, including: time, telephone number, address, cost, name and title of the person you're meeting, and directions.

For projects, put all your notes and ideas in one notebook. Get whichever size is comfortable for you; it can be spiral or ring bound. Write down all of your ideas and information for individual projects in the notebook so that pieces of paper don't become scattered throughout your desk or home.

Another method of recording project ideas is to form an Idea file. You could create several Idea files; for creative work, for business, for home-related projects. The goal is to create the habit of reaching for your notebook whenever you get ideas or information regarding your projects.

A bulletin board can also be used for revolving notes or ideas. Clean off the board once or twice a month to keep old numbers or notes from accumulating.

Maintain a typed list of often used phone numbers in your work area. Post the list over your telephone to make it as useful as possible. With a phone list, you simply glance at the list instead of having to thumb through your phone directory or rolodex.

If you often refer to business cards you collect from colleagues and contacts, buy a business card holder. These holders neatly display the cards. You can alphabetize them or place them in order of need. If you don't want to go to the trouble of sorting your business cards, file them in a folder for future reference. Some people like to keep their collected business cards in a box on the desk, but this is useless clutter. Display your own business cards in a holder on your desk, but other people's cards should be filed in folders according to where you will need them.

Desk

While organizing your work desk, remember that the people who have the cleanest desks are usually the bosses. Is the president's desk ever cluttered? Or left cluttered overnight? Just as you dress for success, have your office and desk dress for success.

So don't store things on top of your desk. Keep your work space clear of everything except the things you use every day. If you always use the Scotch tape dispenser, put it on top. If you don't, keep it in a drawer.

Always have a trash can within reach of your desk. Throwing away papers and keeping your work surface clean is the best way to clear a path through the clutter that accumulates on your desk.

This includes knickknacks. If you must, have only one, or

at most two, knickknacks (pictures, decorative objects, toys) on the top of your desk. Knickknacks are distracting, and where you work is no place to be distracted. Besides, having a jumbled desk can convey a sense of disorganization or tension and frustration that will be reflected in your work.

Clear off your desk every night after you are done working. When you come to your desk fresh the next morning, you won't have to spend your time rearranging things and putting files away. That's a sure opening for procrastination.

After you have cleared off the clutter, you will be able to determine if your desk is big enough for your needs. Often, even after the clutter is cleared away, the problem is simply that your work surface is too small. Obtain a desk to suit your needs. But remember, this is not a free license to store objects on your desk. The larger surface is meant for working.

Supplies

Make certain you have your supplies near your desk. It will keep you from having to get up and down while you're trying to work. Remember not to leave these items on the work surface; put them in a handy drawer instead.

Suggested supplies to keep handy.

Plenty of file holders (the best are the three-quarter tab cut, so the labels can be staggered)
Labels and clear plastic tabs for the folders
Pens and pencils (keep some on your desk in a pencil holder or tray, whichever suits you best)
Paper (in pads and loose bond)
Stationary and envelopes
Overnight and priority postage forms
Tape and dispenser

Stapler, staples, and staple remover
Letter opener, paper clips, pencil sharpener, rubber bands, ruler, and Wite-Out
Scissors
Dictionary
Clock
Phone directory
Reference books
Trash can
Telephone and answering machine

Also, get at least a two-drawer filing cabinet. Even if you only have one drawer worth of files, it's likely you'll expand your files over the years. Besides, that extra drawer makes a handy place to store your supplies.

18 | *Paper Clutter*

Stacks. More stacks. Stacks on stacks. Have you ever caught yourself wondering what your desk looked like underneath all those stacks of paper? Have you ever lost or misplaced an important document? Does the daily mail create havoc in your life?

Getting rid of the paper clutter in your life only takes a few simple, basic techniques in sorting and handling documents and information.

There are four ways to process a piece of paper:

1. You can *throw away* the document.
2. You can take *action* (read, call or write a response).
3. You can *refer* the document to someone else.
4. You can *file* the document for later use.

The best way to deal with incoming documents is to decide how the paper needs to be processed as soon as you receive it. Though constant interruptions are the bane of cluttered time, you should have four separate places—one per "process"—where each document can be quickly tossed until you have the time to deal with it.

Throw Away

When in doubt, save all tax, legal, and financial documents. But if it doesn't have a purpose in your life, throw away the document. Throw away duplicates and out-of-date information as well. Get a big trash can. Don't let a lack of trash space keep you from throwing things out.

Throw away resource information if you haven't got a specific purpose in mind for it *now*. Throw away newspapers, too. After a few days or weeks, they are no longer news.

If you can't stand throw away magazines or newspaper articles, create an Information Reference file where you can write down the name of the periodical, the date, the title of the article, and the subject. Every library keeps microfilm of past periodicals, and it's easy to find and copy this information if you discover you absolutely need it later.

Action

Documents which require action can either be tossed together in a To Do tray or folder, or if you prefer to do some preliminary sorting, divide the documents into separate trays or folders. Suggested categories include: Read, Write/Type, Phone, Record, Order, Copy, Gather Information.

For some people, the Record folder is unnecessary. Small pieces of paper with phone numbers or addresses can be immediately transferred to your phone directory or address book. Then throw away the slip of paper or file it in a backup file. If you keep a rolodex and want to type the address, then put the slip of paper with other documents that you need to type. Other loose papers can be transferred to your calendar in the form of notes to yourself or appointments.

Refer

If it is necessary to *refer* documents to someone else, the recipient's name should be clearly marked on either the document itself or on a Post-It that is attached to the document. Your name and the reason for referral should also be included.

There are several ways to refer the document to the proper person. You can simply toss the marked referral documents in an Out Box; when it is full, you then sort and distribute. or, if you often have documents to pass along, you can have separate Out Boxes labeled with the names of the people you usually refer documents to. If you are using this technique in your home, each member of your family should have a special place, either on individual work space or in a common area where documents or messages can be left.

File

Filing systems are essential to keeping your records and information accessible. Use a filing cabinet or a portable file case. They come in different sizes depending on how many files you own. Everyone needs some files, even if it's only to organize personal documents, leases, financial statements, taxes, etc.

Labeling Files

If you call your car a car, don't label the folder Automobile. Also, don't label a folder with an individual's name if you're dealing with the person's company. Always label according to last name if you do have folders for individuals.

File documents according to the function you plan on using the information for. Don't put an article on cats under Cats if the project you're thinking of using it in is Veterinary Research. You can go to any library and look under Cats for helpful books and articles. Think carefully about each piece of paper before filing it to make certain you are putting it in the place where it will do you the most good.

Make your files broad enough so that they can contain a number of articles and documents. You don't want to create a new file for every new piece of information that comes across your desk. Some of your bigger files can be sub-categorized, depending on which ones are getting the heaviest use.

You can also consider cross-referencing your files. Write a short description of the information and the folder it is filed in on a piece of paper. If you have a large filing system, this can be a time saver.

Organizing Your Files

First, group your files into categories; then alphabetize the folders according to their labels within those larger categories. A few main categories are: Financial, Project Information, Personal, and Business. Each category can be color-coded to aid in refiling the folders, and the categories should be clearly marked within your file cabinet.

The following are some examples of files you are likely to need in each category.

Financial Files:

Banking—savings, checking, credit cards
Housing—rental agreements, mortgages
Contracts
Insurance
Investments—bonds, stocks, real estate loans
Receipts, Warranties, Guarantees
Taxes
Unpaid Bills—utilities, rent, credit cards
Tax Information

Information Files:

Bargains & Sales
Consumer Information
Coupons
Decoration
Entertainment

Gift Ideas
Health & Beauty
Maps and Tourist Information
Restaurants
Services
Travel

Personal Files:

Automobile
Correspondence
Employment—resume, pension
Hobbies
Medical History
School History
Family

Business Files:

Contacts
Correspondence
Expansion
Insurance
Marketing
Personnel
Related Businesses
Vendors

Within each folder itself, the best way to organize information is often by filing date. That is, consistently file your information from either the front or the back of the folder so that the papers are in chronological order of entry.

Another category can be often used files. If you have certain files that you refer to more than others, color code these in a fourth color and put them at the front of your file drawer. But don't use this method unless it is a clear-cut case of ten folders that are used almost every day while the others are seldom referred to.

Maintaining Your Files

File your loose papers depending on the amount you received each week. One rule of thumb is to file when your file tray or folder has more than a dozen or so documents in it.

To make filing faster, after taking action on a document (reading a letter or article) write in pencil or on a post-it the name of the folder the document should be filed in. That way, you won't have to reread the document to determine where it should be filed.

Don't get in the habit of pulling files which you plan on using during a project. That's how files get lost and piles begin to form. Instead, make a note of the files you will need on your calendar or project notes. Also, don't pull a file until you're ready to use it. Otherwise, you'll start to have stacks.

Loose papers can wait to be filed, but folders should always be immediately refiled after you are done with them. That is the only way to keep your filing system useful.

Storage Files

If your files grow quickly, you can maintain a limited number of current files by jotting down the date on the outside of the folder every time you refer to it. This will help you determine when a file should either be put in Storage files or thrown away.

You should go through your filing cabinet once or twice a year. Consider carefully the files you seldom or never refer to. Often the entire folder can be thrown out, if not a large majority of the papers inside of it.

Go through the folders you regularly refer to, as well. There is no reason to keep every piece of paper in a folder, simply because it's been filed. Throw out old articles that you have replaced with updated ones, duplicates, etc.

When a folder gets very full, go through it and pull out

the useless documents and throw them away; or put them in a new folder in the Storage files.

If you are hesitating over throwing out a file, put it in your Storage files. Only very important files, like taxes, financial information, and legal documents should to in storage. Never put Information files in storage.

Storage files can be placed in an inaccessible part of your file drawer, or in boxes. Office supply stores sell sturdy boxes perfect for file folders.

Mail

Is mail part of your clutter problem? For many people, those neat envelopes are an easy thing to ignore—especially junk mail. They pile up in various places, adding to your clutter problem.

Sort the mail into piles for each person in your home or office. Allot a specific place where the mail will be waiting for each person to pick up.

Sort your own mail into magazines, large envelopes, junk mail, and first class. If you find you lose interest after the magazines and first class, then do the junk mail first. After all, that's usually a simple job of tossing it in the trash.

Process the mail into one of the four categories every day: Action, Refer, File, or Throw Away. If you don't process your mail, the next day it qualifies as clutter. It doesn't take long if you keep on schedule; it's only when the mail piles up that it becomes a real chore.

Throw Away

Get rid of most of your mail right after you look at it. Throw it away or recycle it, but don't keep that pamphlet about insurance if you don't plan on buying any in the near future. With mail more than anything else, if you aren't sure, throw the document away. After all, tomorrow you'll get a fresh batch, and insurance notices will be coming to you for the rest of your life. The idea is to free up your environment now and get rid of that clutter.

Action
The Action pile includes the letters you need to write or telephone a response to, the magazines which you place in one pile for reading. Also, change of address notices which you need to enter into your rolodex or address book, appointment confirmations which should be recorded in your calendar, etc.

Refer
The Refer pile should be distributed to the correct person, either by placing a labeled sticky on it and putting it in your Out Box, or by personally conveying it to the person's normal mail drop area.

File
The File pile includes anything that does not need to be dealt with immediately: mail order catalogs, unpaid bills, memos, insurance policies, legal documents, etc.

If you file your correspondence, then do it right after drafting the response. The business correspondence should go in the folder usually labeled by company rather than an individual's name. You can put most of your personal correspondence in one file. For the individuals who send you the most mail, make a file for each. Then you can also put any information regarding this person in the same file.

Computer Clutter

If you own a computer and suffer from paper clutter, it's likely you also suffer from computer clutter.

Keep your computer files as up-to-date as your paper files, otherwise your computer will become cluttered.

When your hard disk is full, the operation of your computer is slowed down and needed byte space is wasted. You also have a harder time finding the useful files in the midst of obsolete ones.

If you've ever lost your hard disk, you've learned the lesson of backing up your documents to floppy every day after you've finished working on them. If you haven't, don't wait for disaster to strike before you learn to back up your files. Hard disks last for an estimated three to five years, but that doesn't mean they don't occasionally conk out after one year or even six months. Get in the habit of backing up your files daily; it's an easy habit you don't even have to think about once you start.

Storage Files

Go through your files regularly, backing up and deleting obsolete files from your hard disk. Check the date on the document screen and transfer the unused documents to floppy with a label of the contents.

Periodically evaluate subdirectories for continued usefulness, as well. If you find you don't use a subdirectory, then copy its contents to floppy and eliminate the entire subdirectory. If two subdirectories are similar and have small menus, then combine the two. This will save time traveling between subdirectories.

If you maintain the files in your computer in this manner, eventually you will acquire piles of floppy disks. Don't keep disk around for years. Just as you occasionally go through your Storage files to eliminate obsolete folders and documents, go through your floppies and reformat the obsolete files.

Remember always to keep financial, tax, and legal information. Save these files onto a new floppy labeled Tax, Financial, or Legal Info, along with the current date.

19 | *Financial Clutter*

Though the visible signs of financial clutter are not as striking as household clutter, it is the worst type of clutter because it is much more important to your livelihood. Losing your bills among the rest of your clutter can result in disaster.

Banking

Keep all your banking statements and deposit slips together. Put these slips of paper in a special place in your purse of briefcase. File them in a Banking folder as soon as you can, to prevent accumulation of clutter in your bag.

Always save your banking statements; they are an important part of your tax information. Some banks have a service whereby they keep your used checks for you for a certain length of time. This is a good service if your canceled checks fill scores of boxes. You don't actually need the check itself if you keep good records in your checkbook. Besides, the number and amount are included in your statement.

Keep a current list of your account numbers and the telephone number of the company in case you need to call. Usually there is a 1-800 telephone number for emergencies and replacements. Numbers you should have on file are:

Bank Accounts—savings and checking
Credit Cards

Driver's License
Social Security Number
Insurance Policies
IRAs
Savings Bonds
Stock Certificates

Bills

Plan on going over your bills once a week, or at the very least, once every two weeks. Don't do it once a month, because bills arrive at different times throughout the month and payment dates will differ. By keeping up to date on your bills you will avoid extra finance charges.

In separate folders, file your receipts, charge carbons, unpaid bills, and paid bills. This will cut down on the confusion in jumbling everything together.

When you receive a bill, check your receipts against the charges to make sure they are correct. Don't assume that your bill is correct; sometimes very large mistakes can happen.

On the part of the bill which you retain for your files, mark the date it was paid and how much the amount was for. This is sometimes easier than keeping all the information in your checkbook.

Total up the amount left in your account after every check. If you don't, you are likely to overdraw your account.

Safe Deposit Box

Everyone should have a safe deposit box in the bank. Anything valuable or irreplaceable should be put in this box. This includes:

Birth and marriage certificates
Divorce papers

Military discharge papers
A copy of your will
Pension plan
Titles to your cars, home, and other property (recreational
vehicle, real estate, etc.)
Passports
Stock certificates, bonds, and certificates of deposit
Valuables, such as jewelry, heirlooms, coins, and stamps.

Make certain you have a list of what your safe deposit box contains in a file marked Safe Deposit Box. Then you won't have to actually go to the bank to find out that your pension plan is not in the box, but filed with your employment records.

If you would rather keep your valuable documents at home, invest in a strong box or fireproof safe. Though this puts your important documents at your fingertips, it is a costly option.

Conclusion

After reading this book you've probably realized that most clutter consists of the loose details in your life. If you break the general mass of clutter down into individual components, it turns out to be a phone call here or there, a messy closet, a pile of papers, a missed appointment...But that's the deceptive nature of clutter. That's how clutter can take over your life—it builds up without you realizing what's happening.

It's true that you don't want to spend a lot of though on the minor details, but clutter takes time from what you really want to be doing. Whether it's objects you acquire or random events that happen, if something is cluttering your life then it's interfering with the things you *do* consider to be important.

So while it can seem like a lot of effort to create habits that will organize your time and space, the results will affect you in ways that aren't immediately apparent. You'll find that when you can control the clutter that comes into your life, it becomes much easier to maintain your clarity of purpose. So get started—unclutter your personal life and reach those goals you set for yourself.

Index

105